Macmillan Modern Dramatists
Series Editors: Bruce and Adele King

Published titles

Reed Anderson, *Federico García Lorca*
Eugene Benson, *J.M. Synge*
Renate Benson, *German Expressionist Drama*
Normand Berlin, *Eugene O'Neill*
Michael Billington, *Alan Ayckbourn*
Roger Boxill, *Tennessee Williams*
John Bull, *New British Political Dramatists*
Dennis Carroll, *David Mamet*
Neil Carson, *Arthur Miller*
Maurice Charney, *Joe Orton*
Ruby Cohn, *New American Dramatists, 1960-1980*
Bernard F. Dukore, *American Dramatists, 1918-1945*
Bernard F. Dukore, *Harold Pinter*
Arthur Ganz, *George Bernard Shaw*
James Gibbs, *Wole Soyinka*
Frances Gray, *John Arden*
Frances Gray, *Noel Coward*
Charles Hayter, *Gilbert and Sullivan*
Julian Hilton, *Georg Büchner*
David Hirst, *Edward Bond*
Helene Keyssar, *Feminist Theatre*
Bettina L. Knapp, *French Theatre 1918-1939*
Charles Lyons, *Samuel Beckett*
Gerry McCarthy, *Edward Albee*
Jan McDonald, *The New Drama 1900-1914*
Susan Bassnett-McGuire, *Luigi Pirandello*
Margery Morgan, *August Strindberg*
Leonard C. Pronko, *Eugene Labiche and Georges Feydeau*
Jeanette L. Savona, *Jean Genet*
Claude Schumacher, *Alfred Jarry and Guillaume Apollinaire*
Laurence Senelick, *Anton Chekhov*
Theodore Shank, *American Alternative Theatre*
James Simmons, *Sean O'Casey*
Ronald Speirs, *Bertolt Brecht*
David Thomas, *Henrik Ibsen*
Dennis Walder, *Athol Fugard*
Thomas Whitaker, *Tom Stoppard*
Nick Worrall, *Nikolai Gogol and Ivan Turgenev*
Katharine Worth, *Oscar Wilde*

Further titles in preparation

MACMILLAN MODERN DRAMATISTS

FEDERICO GARCÍA LORCA

Reed Anderson

Professor, Spanish and Portuguese
Miami University, Oxford, Ohio

MACMILLAN

First published 1984
Reprinted 1989

Published by
MACMILLAN EDUCATION LTD
Houndmills, Basingstoke, Hampshire RG21 2XS
and London
Companies and representatives
throughout the world

Printed in Hong Kong

British Library Cataloguing in Publication Data
Anderson, Reed
Federico García Lorca.—(Macmillan modern dramatists)
1. García Lorca, Federico
2. Dramatists, Spanish—Biography
I. Title
862'.62'0924   PQ6613.A763Z/
ISBN 0-333-31887-0
ISBN 0-333-31888-9 Pbk

Contents

List of Plates   vii

Editors' Preface   ix

1 Life and Literature   1

2 Lorca and the Spanish Theatre   23

3 The Comic Theatre   38

     The Puppet Plays: *The Tragicomedy of Don Cristóbal and Mam'selle Rosita* (1928?) and *Don Cristóbal's Puppet Show* (1931)   40

     The Shoemaker's Wonderful Wife (1933)   48

     The Love of Don Perlimplín and Belisa in the Garden (1933)   57

4 The Granada Plays   65

     Mariana Pineda (1927)   66

     Doña Rosita the Spinster (1936)   73

5 The Three Rural Dramas   87

     Blood Wedding (1933)   90

     Yerma (1934)   103

     The House of Bernarda Alba (1936)   119

6 Innovation and Experiment   133

     As Soon as Five Years Go By (1931)   134

     The Public (1931 and 1936)   143

     Untitled Play (1936)   154

Notes   162

Bibliography   166

Index   169

List of Plates

1. Lorca in the uniform of La Barraca Theatre Company with the Barraca poster behind him. © Aguilar.
2. García Lorca and Margarita Xirgu, 1936. © Bodleian Library.
3. Portrait of Lorca taken in the Garden of San Vicente, Granada, 1935. © Ediciones Destino.
4. Original cast of *The Shoemaker's Wonderful Wife* with Margarita Xirgu as the Wife; costumes and sets by García Lorca, Barcelona, 1930. © Alianza Editorial.
5. Scene from a performance of *The Shoemaker's Wonderful Wife* at King's College, London. © Ediciones Destino.
6. Margarita Xirgu as Mariana in *Mariana Pineda*. Original 1927 production with sets by Salvador Dali. © Alianza Editorial.
7. Original poster for the opening of *Doña Rosita the Spinster*, designed by Grau Sala, 1935. © Ediciones Destino.
8. Margarita Xirgu in the original production of *Doña*

Rosita the Spinster, Barcelona, 1935. © Alianza Editorial.

9. *Blood Wedding*. The Bride and the Bridegroom; the wedding scene, Act II. Directed by José Tamayo, Teatro Bellas Artes, Madrid, 1962. © Bodleian Library.

10. *Blood Wedding*. Leonardo and the Bride in the forest scene, Act III. Directed by José Tamayo, 1962. © Bodleian Library.

11. Yerma and María in *Yerma*. From the original production, 1934, with Margarita Xirgu (right) as Yerma. Teatro Español, Madrid. © Bodleian Library.

12. Final scene of *Yerma;* Yerma's murder of Juan, her husband. Production directed by Luis Escobar, Teatro Eslava, Madrid, 1960. © Bodleian Library.

13. *Yerma*. The Washerwomen (Act II) with Yerma looking on. Production directed by Victor García, with set design by Fabian Puigserver, Teatro de la Comedia, Madrid, 1971. © Bodleian Library.

14. *Yerma*. Yerma discovered by Juan in Dolores the Curess' cave. Directed by Victor García, 1971. © Bodleian Library.

15. *Yerma*. Yerma and the shepherd, Victor. Directed by Victor García, 1971. © Bodleian Library.

16. Costume design drawing by Lorca for La Barraca production of *The Cave of Salamanca* by Cervantes. © Aguilar.

1
Life and Literature

Throughout his adult life, García Lorca spoke frequently and with great pleasure about the profound importance he attributed to his early childhood in the small villages in the countryside near Granada, and later, in the provincial capital city itself. Lorca's father, Federico García Rodríguez, was a wealthy landowner with several substantial holdings in the rich alluvial plain called La Vega de Granada. Having been widowed in his first marriage and left without children, Don Federico's second marriage (of which his family disapproved because of the inferior social and economic background of his bride) was to a school teacher from Granada, Vicenta Lorca Romero. She was an intelligent and cultured young woman, well educated and a lover of music, who had left the capital city to teach school in Fuente Vaqueros, one of the villages in the Vega. The mere fact that she had a profession and a job is an indication of her independence and strength of character. The influence of her personality was to be of the utmost importance for Federico, her oldest son, born in June of

1

1898. 'My childhood', Lorca would recall to an interviewer in 1928, 'consisted of learning reading and music with my mother, and being a rich and overbearing child in a small village.'[1]

At the age of four, García Lorca began attending the local school, and in 1909 the family moved to Granada where they sought the advantages of better schools for all of their four children. Yet the experience of those first ten years in this fertile region of slow rivers and poplar groves, with the snow-capped Sierra Nevada in the distance, seems to have provided Lorca with an inexhaustible well-spring of inspiration and feeling for Spain's rural people and their world. 'My earliest emotions,' Lorca once said, 'are linked to the labour of the countryside . . . my most distant childhood memories have the taste of earth in them. The earth, the countryside have done wonderful things in my life. Small creatures, animals, the rural people, all have a suggestiveness that reaches very few people. I can bring forth all of these things now with the same spirit that they had for me when I was a child' (II, 958–9). And only a year before his untimely death, Lorca echoed this idealised vision, evoking an idyllic experience that indicates the emotional importance of those early years and the values they communicated: 'In all things I love simplicity . . . the simple way of being that I learned as a child off in the village . . . My entire childhood is the village. Shepherds, meadows, sky, solitude, in other words' (I, 977). Even after the family moved to Granada in 1909 they maintained the custom of returning to their country house in La Vega de Granada every summer. And although Lorca lived for the most part in Madrid from about 1920 until his death, he went back regularly to Granada to join his family in the country during holidays and the summer months.

Along with the experience of rural life that Lorca was to

2

carry with him wherever he went – to the city of Granada, to Madrid, Barcelona, New York and to Buenos Aires – there were three great constants in his life that absorbed his creative energies: music, poetry and the theatre. He designed stage settings and costumes and wrote music and lyrics both for his own plays and for the classics of the Spanish theatre that he produced and directed. These artistic interests were fomented and cultivated early in Lorca's life. A servant of the family has left us the impression of Lorca as a young boy with a prodigious memory and a passion for the Spanish folk ballad, able to recite dozens by heart at the age of eight.[2] Thus Lorca trained his literary sensibilities in a popular genre wherein music, dramatic narrative and lyric poetry were all of equal importance. He took piano lessons from his mother, and studied music formally in Almería and in Granada; at home he also learned to play the guitar and to sing Andalusian folk songs from his paternal aunt, Isabel. One of the family's maids recalls Federico constructing an altar, donning an improvised robe and solemnly performing mass, much to the amusement of the other children, and to the good-humoured consternation of the servants. After an itinerant gypsy troupe passed through the town performing traditional puppet theatre Lorca's representation of the mass was quickly replaced by an improvised *guignol* whose characters were based on members of the household.[3] When he was fifteen or sixteen, Lorca bought his own puppet theatre, and his love for this most popular of theatrical forms was to provide the foundation for virtually all of his comic works.

Lorca's career as a student in Granada appears by all accounts to have been unremarkable. He studied law as well as philosophy and letters at the University of Granada and there came into contact with two teachers who were to have a decisive impact on his orientation to literature, and eventually on his intellectual development in general. The first of these mentors was Martín Domínguez Berrueta, a professor of the theory of literature and the arts who organised excursions throughout the country with a focus on cultural history. Lorca took part in two of these tours to the northern and western provinces of Spain, and the important outcome of this travel was his first publication, *Impresiones y paisajes* (*Impressions and Landscapes*), 1918, a book of prose sketches that records his personal experience of the provincial people and places he saw. Another important relationship was with Fernando de los Ríos, a professor of law, one of the leading figures on the socialist left in Granada and a trusted friend and inspiration for many of the young intellectuals of Lorca's generation. De los Ríos urged Lorca to move to Madrid, convinced Lorca's family that this was a reasonable course for their son to take, and arranged for Lorca's acceptance into the famous Residencia de Estudiantes in 1919, where several of his companions from Granada were already living.

The experience of intellectual and artistic community at the Residencia de Estudiantes was extraordinarily rich and most certainly had a crucial influence on Lorca's career. Since 1910 the Residencia had played a definitive role in the education of Spain's liberal youth, serving both as a university residence hall and as a cultural centre. Paul Valery, Louis Aragón, André Breton, H. G. Wells, Igor Stravinsky and Alexander Calder were among those brought to the Residencia for conferences. Juan Ramón Jiménez and Antonio Machado were frequent visitors, and among Lorca's closest companions during those years were fellow residents Salvador Dalí, Luis Buñuel and Rafael Alberti. The Residencia was to be Lorca's Madrid home for nearly ten years, from 1919 until 1928, and Lorca himself played no small part in making that period perhaps the most exciting in the institution's history.[4]

Lorca had arrived in Madrid at the age of 21 with the book of prose sketches, *Impressions and Landscapes*, already to his credit. It was not long, however, before everyone around him was aware of the remarkable poetry that he had been writing at the same time. His friends from Granada took great pleasure in introducing him around in Madrid, and Lorca never failed to produce an unforgettable impression on those he met. He was capable of transfixing an entire group of people even on first meeting with the brilliance of his imagination, the playful spontaneity of his conversation, and the sheer hypnotic force of his energetic and passionate personality. Jorge Guillén, poet and professor of literature, who became a life-long friend of Lorca's after meeting him in 1924, summarises the reaction that many who knew Lorca personally experienced in his presence: 'When I met him for the first time,' Guillén writes, 'he astonished me, and I've never recovered from that astonishment.'[5]

Lorca's consistent practice was to read his work aloud to friends, even in preliminary versions, seeking their reactions, and he seems to have had little ambition to see his poetry in published form. It was the performance of his poetry and not its appearance in print that seemed to be the final fulfilment of his work as a writer. Moreover, the spontaneous pleasure he took in these readings among his friends, and later on in front of more formal audiences, and his genius for recitation have left profound impressions on those who knew him. Lorca's readings, as well as his impromptu performances at the piano of both classical and folk music gained him an ever-widening reputation in Madrid; among those who knew him best, he was called, only partially in jest, the last of the bards. The human presence of the reciter, and the expressive powers of voice and gesture, were all regarded by Lorca as essential to the life of his poetry and he shared with the earliest of the classical Greek dramatists the notion of the unity of lyric poetry with the theatre.

In spite of Lorca's lack of attention to the publication of his work, by 1921 the artist and printer Gabriel García Maroto had succeeded in persuading his young poet friend to organise a collection of the poems he had been writing over the previous several years. The result, *Libro de poemas* (*Book of Poems*), 1921, attracted almost no public or critical attention, although the sympathetic review of one critic, Adolfo Salazar, caught the eye of Juan Ramón Jiménez who then invited Lorca to submit some poems for publication in his new literary journal, *Indice*.

By 1921, however, Lorca had already experienced another public debut, and it is conceivable that the relative silence that greeted the publication of his first book of poems was almost cause for relief in view of the calamitous failure of his first dramatic effort. *El maleficio de la mariposa* (*The Butterfly's Evil Spell*) was a lyric fantasy. It had begun as a poem in dialogue which one of Madrid's most prominent producer-directors, Gregorio Martínez Sierra, had heard Lorca read. Lorca can hardly be faulted for having yielded to the entrepreneur's insistence that the piece should be made into a work for the stage, but neither producer nor playwright was apparently prepared for the noisy altercation between Lorca's supporters and the rest of the audience that took place on the opening night. The play not only closed after its first performance (March 1920), but was barely allowed by the raucous audience to continue until the final curtain. And while Lorca was able to join his friends afterward and laugh about his disastrous theatrical debut, it would be four years

6

before he once again offered a playscript for commercial production.

Even while he was in Madrid during the early 1920s, Lorca's native area of Granada in particular, and the distinctive popular culture of the entire region of Andalusia in general, together constitute the most important source of inspiration for his work. Lorca was working at this time on the poems for his *Poema del cante jondo* (*Deep Song*) and for his *Romancero gitano* (*Gypsy Ballads*), both of which are the most distinctively Andalusian of his poetic works. Moreover, in 1923, Lorca had begun working on his play, *Mariana Pineda*, a romantic tragedy in verse which takes place in Granada and concerns a well-known nineteenth-century heroine in the struggle of liberal Spain against post-Napoleonic Bourbon despotism in that city.

It was about this time as well that Lorca first met the composer Manuel de Falla, who in 1920 had moved permanently to Granada. Two years later they were collaborating on the organisation and production of a festival of 'cante jondo' or 'deep song' devoted to preserving the best and the purest of this most difficult genre of Flamenco singing. Lorca prepared an introductory talk on the 'cante jondo' which he first presented at the Ateneo of Granada in February of 1922, and then at the highly successful festival of music which was held there in June.

Another collaboration with Falla took place during the Christmas season of January 1923, when they jointly produced an elaborate children's show with original music and puppet theatre. The programme consisted of the Medieval Catalan mystery play, *El misterio de los tres reyes de Oriente* (*The Mystery of the Three Wise Men from the East*), in honour of the feast day of the Three Kings, with music by Felipe Pedrell; Stravinsky's music for *L'histoire d'un soldat* provided the background for Lorca's puppet version of Cervantes' novella, *Los dos habladores*, and Lorca's own original puppet play, *La niña que riega la albahaca y el príncipe preguntón* (*The Maiden Who Waters the Sweet Basil and the Inquisitive Prince*) was performed for the first time, with music by Isaac Albéñiz. This programme represented Lorca's first serious chance to work with puppet theatre, and it would lead him toward more elaborate work in the same genre later on.[6] These projects, carried out in Granada at the same time that Lorca was beginning to attract serious attention in Madrid, illustrate the strength of his devotion to the cultural life of his native city.

Granada was also where another of Lorca's most important enterprises took shape, the founding and publication of an independent, *avant-garde* literary review. The publication's mission was deeply rooted in the life of the city itself. It was a labour of love for the city and of hope for the future of its young writers and artists. In their statement of purpose the editors declared war on Granada's lethargic and conservative cultural oligarchy, and openly attacked the mediocrity of the city's officially condoned artistic establishment. *El Gallo* (*The Rooster*) was specifically directed to an Andalusian public, and its purpose was to publish Spain's, and in particular Andalusia's, new writers, and to bring the world of modern art to a city whose tastes (as Lorca declared in his dedication address) had survived unchanged since the 1830s. The first issue contained, among other things, Dalí's *Manifiesto anti-artístico*, and its publication did, in fact, provoke the sharp reaction that the young editors and contributors had anticipated and hoed for. The city's intellectuals were quickly divided into pro- and anti-*Gallo* partisans. The second (and last) issue carried two brief experimental dramatic dialogues by

Lorca: *El paseo de Buster Keaton* (*Buster Keaton Goes for a Stroll*), and *La doncella, el marinero y el estudiante* (*The Maiden, The Sailor and The Student*). This time, the *avant-garde* magazine received comparatively little notice; a few months had been sufficient for the largely conservative city to return to its state of graceful provincial indifference.[7]

Lorca's first full-length work for the theatre is the verse-drama *Mariana Pineda*, a play based on a mixture of local Granadan history and romantic legend. The difficulties Lorca experienced in getting it produced in Madrid, however, reflect the political realities of Spain's cultural life under the military dictatorship of General Miguel Primo de Rivera (1923–30). Gregorio Martínez Sierra, producer-director of Lorca's ill-fated *The Butterfly's Evil Spell* (1920), and his co-producer and leading actress, Catalina Bárcena, had refused *Mariana Pineda* in the spring of 1924. Another of Madrid's most prominent actresses, Josefina Díaz, also apparently had not wished to produce the play.[8] Martínez Sierra at least had initially expressed great enthusiasm for the play when Lorca had given it to him to read, but he had then asked Lorca to make certain changes in the text. When Martínez Sierra turned down the revised version as well, Lorca suffered considerable anxiety over the fortune of the entire project. The refusal certainly had to do with the censorship policies of the conservative Primo de Rivera dictatorship and the fear that the play might be officially interpreted as a liberal manifesto, that is, as a dramatic exposition of the themes of arbitrary tyranny and the revolutionary struggle against its oppressive conditions. The depression that these difficulties caused Lorca may be understood by the fact that he was clearly hoping to gain enough financial success with the play to allow him to establish his economic independence from his family. A well-received production on the Madrid stage would also draw public attention to his work as a dramatist just at the moment when he was also becoming widely recognised and celebrated as one of Spain's most promising young lyric poets. Such a success would obviate the need to steal time from his creative work in the pursuit of ways to earn an independent living (Lorca had briefly entertained the thought of seeking an academic position), and the play's acceptance would give him the excuse he needed to leave Granada and move back to Madrid in order to oversee its staging. Although in a sense *Mariana Pineda* was a homage to Granada, it is also true that Lorca very much wanted to leave the provincial capital and solidify his independence from his family with some kind of proof that he could indeed make a career as a writer.

Finally, after an exasperating wait of several months, Cataluña's most prominent and influential actress and producer, Margarita Xirgu, scheduled *Mariana Pineda* for production during her company's autumn (1927) season in Barcelona. Margarita Xirgu was an artist with a keen and bold political sense who devoted herself both professionally and personally to the cause of the political left in Spain during the 1920s and 1930s. She became one of Lorca's most trusted friends, and played a crucial role in the promotion of his works for the theatre during the 1930s, and also after his death. When at last *Mariana Pineda* went into production, Lorca was at work on projects of such a different kind that he was again apprehensive about the prospects for this 'romantic' drama on the Madrid stage. The moderate success of *Mariana Pineda* quieted Lorca's concerns about his second 'debut' on the commercial stage. The play, in fact, had two runs in 1927, one in Barcelona, during the summer, with sets by Lorca's close friend Salvador Dalí, and the other in Madrid during October.

While much of Lorca's personal popularity in Spain and

abroad was in response to the poetry he published in his *Canciones* (*Songs*), 1927, and to the unprecedented sensation caused by his *Romancero gitano* (*Gypsy Ballads*), 1928, (*Songs*), 1927, he had to struggle with the tendency of the public to regard him only as an 'Andalusian' poet, or even more restrictively, as a kind of gifted folk poet of Spain's gypsy culture. Typically, Lorca had put off or all but forgotten about the publication of both these works of poetry, and when they finally did appear in print, he had already moved on to other undertakings of a substantially different kind. In a letter to his close friend, Sebastiá Gasch, he said of the *Gypsy Ballads*, 'naturally the mummies haven't understood my book at all, even though they claim to. And, in spite of that, I no longer have the least interest in it, or nearly so. It died in my hands in the gentlest way. My poetry is now beginning to take off in an even more personal direction' (II, 1219–20). So that while Lorca was coping with the overnight celebrity he had acquired with the *Gypsy Ballads*, he was also plunging into what he considered at the time to be far more compelling undertakings, among which were works for the stage. There is evidence in Lorca's correspondence with Dalí's sister Ana María, for instance, that he had finished a full-length play called *Iphigenia* in the fall of 1927, but the whereabouts of the manuscript remains a mystery. In October of 1928, Lorca addressed the Ateneo of Granada with his important essay on the nature and aesthetics of poetry, 'Imaginación, inspiración y evasión' ('Imagination, Inspiration and Escapism'). Also under way at this time were several of his most outstanding comic works for the stage: *El amor de don Perlimplín con Belisa en su jardín* (*The Love of Don Perlimplín With Belisa in The Garden*), and the farces for puppets, *Los títeres de cachiporra: La tragicomedia de don Cristóbal y la Señá Rosita* (*The Tragicomedy of Don*

Cristóbal and Mam'selle Rosita);[9] and *Retablillo de don Cristóbal* (*Don Cristóbal's Puppet Show*). Finally, the first half of 1929 saw two important theatre production projects by Lorca. During the winter, an effort to present *Don Perlimplín* was stopped by government censors and in late April a successful performance of *Mariana Pineda* at last took place in Granada.

The years 1927 to 1929 appear to have been ones of intense work, filled with diverse projects, but also marked by an unusual degree of personal stress. While Lorca was constantly concerned with establishing himself in the theatre, he had suffered some setbacks and only modest successes in that area. But he also experienced a rather severe personal crisis during the winter and spring of 1929. The poet himself says almost nothing about it, and even his intimate friends refer to it only in the most circumspect terms. Whatever the details, there seems to have been a need at this time to transcend some kind of emotional difficulties, and the answer was a somewhat precipitous decision on Lorca's part to accompany his old mentor and trusted friend, don Fernando de los Ríos, who had been exiled by the Primo de Rivera government, on a trip to the United States. Thus, in June 1929, Lorca arrived in New York City, not knowing a word of English, and began his stay at Columbia University where he would reside until his departure for a two-month visit to Cuba in March and April of the following year.

The New York experience was for Lorca profoundly disturbing, stimulating, and extraordinarily productive. He was able to revise his initial version of *Don Perlimplín*, but he was also in the process of writing and planning at least three other works for the stage: *La Zapatera prodigiosa* (*The Shoemaker's Wonderful Wife*), *Así que pasen cinco años* (*As Soon As Five Years Go By*),[10] and *El público* (*The*

Public). At the same time, this metropolis, with its world-wide financial power and its unspeakable squalor, became for Lorca a terrible and fascinating symbol of the dehumanising effects of modern technological civilisation. The October 1929 stock market crash and the ensuing panic and economic crisis dramatised already existing contradictions. The horror, rage and wonder Lorca experienced upon seeing and feeling the consequences this civilisation had on the human inhabitants of that city gave rise to a new poetic voice which was deeply subjective, and at the same time, militantly opposed to the injustice and violence that this materialistic society worked on its oppressed classes. Lorca's *Poet in New York* remains as a monumental work of outrage, and a relentless exploration of the poet's own subjective posture as a witness to this degradation of the human spirit. In March of 1930, Lorca travelled to Cuba at the invitation of the Institución Hispano-Cubana in Havana where he delivered several of his already famous lectures and read from his literary works. The visit to Cuba turned out to be thoroughly recuperative after Lorca's frequently stressful stay in the United States. When he returned to Spain in June, he went directly to Granada where he spent the rest of the summer and part of the autumn.

The year following Lorca's return to Spain was a crucial one in Spain's modern political history. With the end of the Primo de Rivera dictatorship (1923–30), Spanish Republicans began the work of drawing together the country's left and liberal forces in anticipation of the nationwide municipal elections to be held in April of 1931. The Republican victory in the April elections led immediately to the abdication of King Alfonso XIII and the declaration of the Second Spanish Republic. The next five years – the last five of Lorca's life – were years of intense political struggle as a liberal-Republican government attempted to legislate measures that would bring about the social and economic change that the forces on the left were calling for. From 1934 on, that same government had to take action against monarchist and proto-fascist forces from the right that were growing ever more bold in their attempts to subvert the Republic's efforts at programmes of liberal reform. Spain's seriously uneven economic development had seen the growth of a significant industrial proletariat in the cities, while in the countryside, the land was either in vast and unproductive estates in the South, or small holdings in the North that were neither commercially viable nor in many cases even sufficient to sustain those who lived on them. This severe rural poverty was accompanied by an illiteracy rate in the 1930s of somewhere between 30 and 50 per cent.[11]

In such an uncertain and highly politicised atmosphere as Republican Spain's winter of 1930–31, it is perhaps not surprising that the opening run of Lorca's light-hearted farce, *The Shoemaker's Wonderful Wife* lasted only a week, even with the collaboration of Margarita Xirgu and the growing public acclaim that Lorca was enjoying at the time. Throughout the spring and summer of 1931, Lorca continued the private and public readings of the poems that were later to be collected into *The Poet in New York* and were accompanied by their gradual publication in various of the country's leading journals. Another long-delayed publication of a poetry collection took place in the Spring of 1931 (*El poema del cante jondo*, *The Poem of the Deep Song*), whose manuscript had been set aside since about 1921 when Lorca had first written it.

But the most important single moment in Lorca's career as a dramatist came in November of 1931 when he announced to his close friends an idea that he had conceived for the founding of an itinerant theatre company that would carry the great works of the classical Spanish theatre to the provincial capital cities of Spain, and into the villages of the isolated countryside. It would be free to the public and performed in the open air, a revival of the venerable institution of the travelling theatre show, but this time with the purpose of stimulating and edifying the cultural appetites of people who were virtually without formal education of any kind. Cervantes, Lope de Vega, Calderón de la Barca, and Tirso de Molina would be brought before audiences that Lorca was convinced would have an appreciation of the value of these works superior to that of the bourgeois public he faced again and again in Spain's major cities. The new company would be called La Barraca (The Caravan); its constitution spelled out its goals:

> The University Theatre (this was its official designation) proposes to carry out the artistic renovation of the Spanish stage. For this purpose, the classics will be employed as the educators of popular taste; our activities, which will be carried out in the provincial capitals where this renovation is most drastically needed, will also be directed to the diffusion of theatre among the rural masses who have been altogether deprived of theatre through the ages.[12]

The conception of this unique theatre project was Lorca's personal response as an artist to the progressive political and cultural ideals of the newly established Republican government. At the same time, it represented an opportunity to put into practice ideas that Lorca had long held concerning the need for profound reforms in the Spanish theatre – reforms that would address and cultivate entirely new audiences for drama, and thereby stimulate the production of new plays. The appointment of Lorca's old and trusted friend, Fernando de los Ríos, as the Republican Government's Minister of Education seemed to ensure that this idea would find both financial and ideological support at the highest levels.

Lorca was the new company's artistic director, and his assistant was his long-time friend, Eduardo Ugarte. Between them they selected the repertoire, organised and judged tryouts, trained the amateur actors and actresses, and prepared the acting scripts of the works to be performed. They oversaw scenic design, costuming and all the physical details of assembling a theatre caravan whose productions could be set up and struck with maximum efficiency, sometimes in a matter of hours. For three years Lorca devoted himself tirelessly to the work of adapting and producing classical Spanish plays for La Barraca. Actual performances were often carried on under very trying and unexpected circumstances in the rural towns and provincial capitals they visited. Uncertain weather was a constant factor in the company's life, as was the threat of politically-inspired opposition to this Republican government-sponsored organisation in some of the areas they played.

When, in 1934, his writing and the production of his own major plays were beginning to make unprecedented demands on his time, Lorca gradually withdrew from full participation in La Barraca. The summer of 1935 was the final tour of the theatre with which Lorca would be in any way involved. The importance of this entire period was made clear by a simple but revealing statement that Lorca made to an interviewer in 1934:

It is amazing the concentration, the intelligence and the

unity with which these students are working. A professional company would be hard put to come up with the kind of results they are achieving . . . and with all of the rehearsals and experimentations, I feel that I am becoming trained as a director, a difficult and slow apprenticeship. I am stimulated to use this experience to go on to do many other things. (II, 964)

In contrast to the first ten years of Lorca's residence and work in Madrid (approximately 1920–30), when it was his poetry that primarily accounted for his public and critical acclaim, the 1930s were marked by Lorca's emergence as the single most important force in the Spanish theatre. From 1930 to 1936, he was constantly occupied with his writing for the stage, his adaptations for and direction of the repertory of La Barraca, and the production and direction of his own works in Madrid, Barcelona and, during the 1933–34 season, in Buenos Aires. The plays that were written and that reached commercial production during the first half of the 1930s are in fact those that established Lorca's national as well as international reputation as a playwright. *Bodas de sangre* (*Blood Wedding*), *Yerma*, and *La casa de Bernarda Alba* (*The House of Bernarda Alba*) (although the latter was never produced during Lorca's lifetime) are all products of the 1930s, that is, the period after Lorca's trip to the United States, and during the years of the Second Spanish Republic.

It is difficult to point to any kind of linear, chronologically ordered evolution in Lorca's writing for the stage. Naturally, his more mature and substantial works demonstrate a synthesis of themes and a mastery of stagecraft that we may be tempted to contrast with his lighter and more occasional pieces. Nevertheless, if we look closely at the pattern of Lorca's productivity during the last eight years of

17

his life, we discover the most disparate of imaginable combinations of writing and directing projects, and actual stage productions. For example, the bright Andalusian farce, *The Shoemaker's Wonderful Wife*, was probably written for the most part in New York and Cuba at the same time Lorca was chronicling the horrors of a decaying urban culture in his New York poems. This was the same general period (1929–30) when Lorca read to friends in Havana the finished versions of his most difficult and formally daring dramas, *As Soon As Five Years Go By* and *The Public*. Then, the same theatre season that saw the opening of the peasant tragedy *Blood Wedding* (1933), had also seen the opening of *The Love of Don Perlimplín*, perhaps Lorca's most successful and substantial comic work. In 1935, the revision and definitive production of *The Shoemaker's Wonderful Wife*, under Lorca's own direction in Madrid, coincided with the lengthy run of the lyric tragedy, *Yerma*, and the preparation of two of Lorca's most successful comic pieces for puppets, performed at the National Book Fair in Madrid, May 1935. By June of that same year Lorca had also read the first complete version of his tragic-comic *Doña Rosita da soltera* (*Doña Rosita The Spinster*), which had its debut with Margarita Xirgu in the leading role in Barcelona in December 1935. Meanwhile, Lorca's brilliant work at adapting the classics of the Spanish Golden Age theatre to the modern stage for La Barraca was occupying his attention from 1932 to 1935.

In addition, there are several intriguing mysteries surrounding the projects that Lorca may have been working on during the last two years of his life. He mentioned to friends, for instance, that he was planning to write a 'political tragedy', and a tragedy concerning 'soldiers who refuse to go to war'.[13] He spoke as well of a drama he called *La sangre no tiene voz* (*Blood Has No Voice*), whose theme was incest, and he mentioned a projected Biblical trilogy, one of whose elements would be a play called either *El drama de las hijas de Loth* (*The Drama of Lot's Daughters*), or *La destrucción de Sodoma* (*The Destruction of Sodom*). In the case of these, as well as of several other titles that Lorca mentioned to friends, it is impossible to know whether they refer to sketches, outlines, finished drafts, or whether they merely refer to ideas for future works to which Lorca had already attached tentative titles. What was by all accounts astounding to those who knew Lorca well was the number and the variety of projects that he would be thinking about and writing or producing at any given moment.

If anything can be said to have been constant throughout all of this remarkably productive period of Lorca's career, it is his dedication to experimentation with all the possibilities of the stage in an attempt to extend the expressive range of the Spanish theatre, to cultivate new audiences in new places, and to educate and challenge the theatre-going public in the country's principal cultural centres, Madrid and Barcelona. It turned out that his influence also extended to the theatre of Buenos Aires as the result of his triumphal tour there in the winter of 1931–32, and at the time of his death acclaim for his work was spread throughout the Spanish-speaking world.

Lorca's importance as a playwright and his most significant contribution to the Spanish stage consists in the fruition of a particular concept of theatre. Stated in the simplest terms, Lorca's work was to transform the level of dramatic discourse (dialogue, characterisation, stagecraft) from the stylised pseudo-naturalism that had prevailed in commercial houses since the nineteenth century. 'Theatre', he told an interviewer, 'is poetry that rises up off the page and becomes human. And in so becoming, it speaks and

shouts, it weeps and despairs. Theatre needs for its
characters to come on stage dressed in the garb of poetry,
and at the same time with their bones and their blood
showing through' (II, 1015).

The years 1935 and 1936 saw the virtually constant
collaboration of Lorca with the great Catalan actress and
impresario, Margarita Xirgu. *Yerma* was written expressly
with her in mind for the leading role; the second run of
Blood Wedding (this time in Barcelona) had Xirgu in the
role of the Mother, and Lorca felt that this was the
definitive performance of his work. Xirgu took the leading
role in *Doña Rosita the Spinster* in its December 1935
opening in Barcelona. Also in 1935, an official Spanish
cultural tour of Italy was scheduled where Xirgu's company
was to present works by Lope de Vega and where Lorca
was to read his own poetry and deliver several talks. The
tour was cancelled, however, in protest over Mussolini's
invasion of Abyssinia, and a proclamation condemning this
act and in support of the people of Abyssinia was signed a
few days later by Lorca and several other prominent
Spanish cultural figures. An extensive tour of Mexico by
Lorca, Margarita Xirgu and her company was also in the
final stages of planning in April of 1936, and Lorca had
already submitted his resignation from the directorship of La
Barraca because of this and the many other obligations that
required his attention. By the spring of 1936 Lorca had
achieved substantial public recognition for his poetry and
his theatre both in Spain and in the Spanish-speaking world
abroad. To English-speaking audiences, he was known
mainly through translations of his poetry. During the last
two years of his life, Lorca also figured prominently among
those Spanish artists and intellectuals who in many different ways were taking public positions opposing the rise
of international fascism and of its sympathisers in Spain.

His identification with the political left was clear, and it was to prove dangerous to Lorca once the political struggle had become polarised and erupted into armed conflict with the military insurrection led by General Francisco Franco in the summer of 1936. In the vindicative violence that swept Granada during the first weeks of the rightist take-over, there can be little doubt that Lorca was regarded by those who seized power as one of the most widely-known personalities on the 'enemy' side.[14]

The bare facts of Lorca's tragic death are known, although details are scant. On 23 June 1936, Lorca read the completed manuscript of *The House of Bernarda Alba* to a large gathering of friends in Madrid. *As Soon As Five Years Go By* was in rehearsal with the Club Anfistora theatre group, and its opening was projected for later that summer. On 16 July, however, just two days before the beginning of what was to become the Spanish Republic's protracted battle against international fascism, Lorca returned to his home in Granada to be with his family. The socialist mayor of that city, Manuel Montesinos, was Lorca's brother-in-law, and when Granada fell into the hands of the Franco-led insurrectionists, widespread arrests of liberals and leftists were quickly carried out. On 3 August, after the city had been occupied by fascist troops, Montesinos was executed. Even so, at that time Lorca felt no need to hide, but when two armed men came to the family's country house in search of a worker known to be a 'red', they encountered Lorca there instead. The men are said to have struck Lorca several times and to have threatened him. This unnerving incident persuaded Lorca and his family that he should in fact seek a place of refuge from this campaign of terror with its vindicative arrests and summary executions. Lorca then began a period of seclusion at the city home of a friend whose right-wing sympathies, it was thought, would guarantee his safety. Nevertheless, it was to this very house that one of the fascist police groups called the Black Squads came and 'arrested' Lorca, taking him to a make-shift prison outside the city. On the morning of 19 August 1936, he was taken out to a roadside ravine and, probably along with several others, executed and buried anonymously in a mass gravesite.

2
Lorca and the Spanish Theatre

In 1930 one of Spain's leading editors and critics wrote, 'Probably the only contemporary writer who holds any authority over the public is Benavente. His works might not please the opening night critics, but he is allowed to say anything he wants to say and in whatever form he chooses.'[1] The extraordinary intelligence and productivity of the Nobel Prize-winning dramatist Jacinto Benavente (1866–1954), enabled him virtually to dominate the commercial theatre in Spain for over three decades. Benavente's own ascent had begun just at the turn of the century when another Nobel Prize-winner, José de Echegaray, enjoyed the same public adulation and box office success that Benavente was soon to attain. Echegaray's tendentious verse melodramas whose sensationalistic treatments of such themes as alcoholism, incest, adultery and madness always justified themselves with the conventionality of their moral view, gave way in a relatively short time to Benavente's far more sophisticated, polished and witty comedies and tragi-comedies that began to capture the attention of the wealthy and conservative urban bourgeoisie. His sly satires of the same social class that constituted his most avid following always operated within acceptable bounds, and when he did push into mildly controversial areas, it was always with the confidence that he could take his audience with him and bring them back again at the end of the play without any profound disturbance of their conservative values. On the other hand, Benito Pérez Galdós – Spain's major novelist of the nineteenth and early twentieth centuries – whose plays were realistic representations of the lives of the politically liberal middle class, never achieved real commercial success. Similarly, the intense psychological dramas of the novelist, poet and philosopher, Miguel de Unamuno, and the formal experiments of the brothers Antonio and Manuel Machado, and of José Martínez Ruiz (Azorín) failed to interest the public and failed to inspire the interest of other dramatists who might have refined and perfected some of the innovations in theme and technique suggested by this body of work.

Superficially, the situation of the Spanish theatre during the 1920s was paradoxical. The sophisticated works of Benavente and Eduardo Marquina (1879–1946) drew faithful audiences from the traditional cultured bourgeosie, and Pedro Muñoz Seca, Carlos Arniches and the brothers Alvarez Quintero, along with a host of imitators, produced colourful and widely popular works full of typecast characters drawn from the provinces and from the streets of the urban working-class neighbourhoods. Theatre as a commercial enterprise was flourishing, and yet there was constant public discussion of crisis, decadence and stagnation. In the final analysis, of course, it was this very commercial success that had brought about the extreme reluctance to innovate or experiment. In the opinion of its harshest critics the theatre was an art form that was capable of exerting a serious cultural, moral and ideological influence on public life, and the theatre that was monopolising the commercial stage had relinquished all such responsibility in favour of pleasing conservative audiences. Playwrights either offered innocuous entertainments, or their works simply represented repeated affirmations of the political, moral and cultural ideologies of their patrons. The most significant challenge to the prevailing conservative ideological hegemony was mounted by a dramatist whose plays were only rarely produced, and then only to audiences of aficionados in non-commercial theatre clubs.

Ramón María del Valle-Inclán (1866–1936) was unquestionably the most radical of the playwrights who opposed the theatre establishment during the late 1920s and 1930s. In line with the best of the European expressionist artists, Valle-Inclán's mature theatre represented a bitter and satirical attack on the hypocritical idealism and the moralising sentimentality of the bourgeois playwrights who dominated the Spanish stage. His *esperpentos* are grotesque parodies of the moral views of the ruling classes. Masculine honour, militarism, patriotism, and the unquestioning defence of the throne and the Catholic Church are the favourite targets of his festive but dark satires. While the material and political interests of the ruling triumvirate composed of the clergy, the military and the monarchist oligarchy were desperately being shored up under the proto-fascist military dictatorship of General Miguel Primo de Rivera from 1923 until 1930, Valle-Inclán was writing his most aggressive works for the theatre. It is hardly surprising that they were almost never produced.

Aside from the obvious political difficulties presented by Valle-Inclán's subversive vision of Spanish society and history, the staging that he called for in his works went beyond the imagination and the technical abilities of most of Spain's contemporary directors for commercial theatre. He incorporated both music and dance into his dramas, often calling for drastic changes of scene over the course of rapid sequences of vignettes; the scenes themselves were often macabre and grotesque, some requiring difficult supernatural effects to be created. His characters ranged from members of the decadent rural aristocracy to the most miserable of the indigent masses that populated Spain's towns and countryside. He also portrayed with great irreverence figures out of Spain's recent political past, such as the profligate queen, Isabel II. The characters' language was crude, obscene and often filled with vulgar parodies; it was on the whole a mockery and a violent attack on the theatrical rhetoric and bland stylisation of 'colourful' popular speech that was heard constantly on the Madrid stage. Although Lorca's critical vision is less mordant, satirical and aggressive than Valle-Inclán's, the vast possibilities for the use of the stage, the human voice and the body that were suggested by Valle-Inclán's dramaturgy undoubtedly were a stimulating example for Lorca as he developed his own style during the late 1920s and 1930s.

Given these general conditions in the Spanish theatre during the first decades of the twentieth century, the importance of Gregorio and María Martínez Sierra and their directorship of Madrid's Teatro Eslava becomes even more apparent. The Teatro Eslava and its company constituted the only art theatre that Madrid had for nearly a decade. As its director, Gregorio Martínez Sierra cultivated the talents of several of Spain's most outstanding young scenic designers, and the company's repertory was

Editors' Preface

The *Macmillan Modern Dramatists* is an international series of introductions to major and significant nineteenth- and twentieth-century dramatists, movements and new forms of drama in Europe, Great Britain, America and new nations such as Nigeria and Trinidad. Besides new studies of great and influential dramatists of the past, the series includes volumes on contemporary authors, recent trends in the theatre and on many dramatists, such as writers of farce, who have created theatre 'classics' while being neglected by literary criticism. The volumes in the series devoted to individual dramatists include a biography, a survey of the plays, and detailed analysis of the most significant plays, along with discussion, where relevant, of the political, social, historical and theatrical context. The authors of the volumes, who are involved with theatre as playwrights, directors, actors, teachers and critics, are concerned with the plays as theatre and discuss such matters as performance, character interpretation and staging, along with themes and contexts.

BRUCE KING
ADELE KING

unique not only for its attention to the international classics, but because it was willing to risk the inclusion of many of Spain's young, unknown dramatists. The Teatro Eslava was responsible for the presentation of works by Shakespeare, Molière, Goldoni, Dumas, Ibsen, Shaw and Barrie to Spanish audiences between 1917 and 1924,[2] while at the same time, it was Martínez Sierra's initiative that brought Lorca's ill-fated *Butterfly's Evil Spell* to the stage in 1920. And while both Lorca and his producer were distinctly mistaken in their estimation of the receptivity of the Madrid public for such fanciful and poetic theatre, there was no other impresario in the capital at the time who would have taken the risk of encouraging and producing such a piece.

From about 1930 on, Lorca spoke constantly of his dramatic work, gave interviews and frequently addressed both formal and informal gatherings of friends and theatre people. Aside from the plays themselves, the record of these statements constitutes the only body of information we have concerning Lorca's aesthetic ideas. But even from this fairly scant evidence, we can see nonetheless that Lorca was a careful and detailed analyst of drama in general, and of his own work in particular.

At the foundation of Lorca's effort to revolutionise the theatre of his day was his conviction that great drama had been and always would be poetic drama. 'The theatre that has always endured is theatre written by poets,' Lorca said in 1935, 'and theatre has been great in proportion to the greatness of the poet. I am not talking about the lyric poet, of course, but the dramatic poet' (II, 982). More precisely, Lorca regarded the theatre as a form that was vitally linked to people's lives, and that was capable of showing them the truth about what they experienced:

Federico García Lorca

> The theatre is one of the most expressive and useful vehicles for the edification of a country's people, and a barometer that marks the country's greatness or decline. . . . The theatre is a school of tears and laughter and an open tribunal where people can place outmoded or erroneous mores on trial and explain through living examples the eternal standards of the human heart and feelings. (I, 1178)

In the 1920s and 1930s in Spain, this barometer of national cultural climate was marking a particularly low point, according to Lorca. On the whole, Lorca's reactions to the theatre in Madrid were articulated discreetly and constructively, and with a view to the ways in which his own work constituted a coherent response to the state of affairs he was criticising.

Lorca certainly understood the structural and economic base of the problem that was stifling innovation and discouraging an entire generation of young writers and actors. A commercial theatre, competing for audiences in an open marketplace, and governed by no higher motive than that of financial success, was a theatre doomed to sterility. Consequently the theatre had lost its 'authority' as an institution of culture, and had relinquished what for Lorca was its most essential responsibility, which was to move people, and thus to teach them about themselves and about life. 'The theatre has lost its authority,' Lorca stated in a 1934 address,

> because day by day a great imbalance has developed between art and business. The theatre needs money . . . but this should be only half of the picture. The other half is refinement, beauty, craft, sacrifice in the interest of a higher goal of feeling and culture. I am not talking about

the art theatre, or experimental theatre, because they will always show losses rather than profits; I am talking about the regular everyday theatre, the income-producing theatre where [we] must require a minimum of decorum and never allow it to lose sight of its artistic, its educative function. (I, 1171)

Although Lorca characterised himself as an 'ardent *apasionado* of the theatre of social action', by this he did not mean political theatre, or 'agit-prop', though he was aware of the existence of both. Rather, he was referring to theatre with a specific and clearly understood historical relationship to its public. Lorca came to believe that a major part of the renovation of the Spanish stage would take place, not only through the reorientation of traditional audiences, but through the cultivation of new audiences as well. The most serious problem he saw with the established theatre was not so much one of form as it was one of receptivity – the problem of a public that would not tolerate works that challenged them to deal with moral questions. At the same time, Lorca was convinced that members of Spain's working class and rural peasantry could be brought to a high level of appreciation of theatre through the experience of seeing the very best theatre performed and produced with imagination, seriousness and discipline.

Lorca literally created the means to carry out these ideas in practice, and at the same time, he significantly broadened and perfected his own skills as a creator of theatre in all its phases. His travelling company, La Barraca, had the purpose of experimenting with various different styles of performance and staging in order to gauge the receptivity of popular audiences. The repertoire would consist of the classics of the Spanish sixteenth and seventeenth centuries but, for instance, with one version that attempted to reproduce the original, realistic style of the play, and another that would be simplified in its staging, using modern costumes, techniques and effects, at least as far as would be permitted by the company's resources. Lorca's idea, as he put it, was 'to bring these works up out of the depths of the libraries, to snatch them away from the scholars and return them to the sunlight and the fresh air of the villages' (II, 898). The audiences would be experiencing the revival of what was once, according to Lorca's idealistic interpretation of the situation, a vital part of their culture.

By all accounts, Lorca's insight concerning the receptivity of provincial audiences proved accurate. In some areas of the provinces, political forces that were opposed to the sponsoring Republican government would foment suspicion or hostility among townspeople towards La Barraca and its youthful ensemble of actors, artists and technicians. But the seriousness and respect with which the plays were presented invariably earned the admiration of the audiences by the end of the performances. Lorca observed very carefully and commented on the rapt attention and the awed silence with which the residents of some of Spain's most backward villages would view the works of Lope de Rueda, Lope de Vega, Cervantes, Tirso de Molina and Calderón de la Barca. 'We have come across only one public that is not enthusiastic about our work,' he told an interviewer,

> [and that is] the middle class, the frivolous and materialistic bourgeoisie. Our audiences, those who truly can grasp the art of the theatre, are on the two extremes: the cultured and university-educated classes, or those who are artistically and intellectually self-educated, and the masses, the poorest and most uncultivated *pueblo*, who are still uncontaminated, virginal,

fertile ground that senses the stirrings of every kind of pain and the playfulness of every kind of wit. (II, 952)

What seemed to Lorca so remarkable about these unsophisticated spectators was their apparent disposition, their willingness to view drama as both artificial and conventional in form, and to seek analogies with real life, not at the level of faithful mimetic reproduction of reality, but at the level of ideology and truth. Lorca once described a visit La Barraca made to the village of Toboso in the province of La Mancha where they presented a play by Calderón de la Barca with what seem to have been quite extravagant costumes. Lorca remarked on the reception of the play by the rural audience as follows:

The characters in the play had metal wigs, silver wigs and others of different materials; green beards; gentlemen dressed in costumes with huge shoulder pads. Totally unrealistic by common-sense standards. And in spite of it all – and what a reassurance it was – everything was understood right down to the smallest details by that audience that was being introduced that way for the first time to Calderón. Not one of them found anything that conflicted with his/her own sense of reality. And it was because we, with our green beards, with our copper hair, with our oversized shoulder pads, we were telling the truth. And the people of the countryside have their hearing and their souls perfectly fashioned to receive, store and ripen that truth that we gave them.[3]

It was precisely this dialectic involving the representation of ideology or ethos by means of an illusory experience created through the skilful construction of a complex dramatic artifice that was at the centre of Lorca's life-long fascination with the theatre.

La Barraca, then, was a unique opportunity to experiment with productions before the widest imaginable range of audiences, and its goals were consonant with Lorca's desire to see his theatre projects form part of the cultural lives of great numbers of people. Art and literature for Lorca were primarily social, and as often as not to be experienced collectively, in performance, as part of an audience.

There was scarcely a single detail in the world of the contemporary theatre in Spain that escaped Lorca's notice. At the same time he undertook his truly daring enterprise with La Barraca, Lorca was also engaged in the establishment of theatre clubs in the cities, whose mission would be to produce works that the commercial theatre would not risk. A few private groups already existed, but their programmes, according to Lorca, were facile and old-fashioned, serving as a pretext for social gatherings among a small élite. In contrast to these amateur clubs, Lorca's purpose was to bring together writers, actors and directors who would profit from one another's talent and ideas in producing plays free from the constraints of having to guarantee financial success to an impresario. The goal, as Lorca saw it, would be to create art, but most important of all, art accessible to everyone. Once again, Lorca brings up the common enterprise characteristic of responsible theatre, wherein not only does the training and exposure of young talent take place, but where audiences are at the same time educated and encouraged to the new level of critical receptivity that would be demanded by contemporary plays and advanced production methods. Lorca wrote, adapted and produced works of his own specifically for these new theatre groups; *The Shoemaker's Wonderful Wife* and *The Love of Don Perlimplín* were both featured in April of 1933 on the programme for the Club Anfistora (later known as the Club Teatral de Cultura), just a month before *Blood Wedding* had its successful premiere performance on the commercial stage in Barcelona.

During Lorca's triumphant visit to Buenos Aires in the winter of 1933–34, the full range of his extraordinary talent and craftsmanship was displayed. As a result, the recognition he had begun to achieve in Spain was enhanced throughout the Spanish-speaking world. Lorca returned to Spain in the spring of 1934 having become without question the dominant new force in the world of the Spanish theatre, and the 'authority' of his dramaturgy was beginning to take a firm hold on audiences and professionals alike.

Lorca's thinking about the theatre and its relationship to the public nevertheless continued to evolve. Moreover, as the reality of Fascist power in Europe became more stark and as conflict among forces on Spain's own political right and left approached the point of crisis, Lorca was compelled to examine his own position as an artist. Concerning his theatre, Lorca spoke increasingly in terms of 'these times we are experiencing' and he struggled to ensure that his work should continue to bear the relationship to history that he believed was essential to any authentic and universal art. 'This whole idea of art for art's sake,' he declared in 1936 in one of his final and most revealing interviews,

is something that would be cruel if fortunately it weren't such an affectation. No real person believes anymore in that nonsense about pure art, about art for the sake of art. At this dramatic moment in history the artist must weep and laugh with his people. He must lay aside his bouquet of lilies and plunge up to his waist into the mud to help those who are searching for lilies. (II, 1019–20)

'I know very well how to write semi-intellectual plays,' he said in 1935, 'but that's not important. In our times, poets must open their veins for others. For that reason . . . I have given myself over exclusively to the theatre, which allows me a more direct contact with the masses' (II, 978). The universal principle that governed Lorca's work for the stage, then, would be this:

[That] any theatre will only continue to be authentic as it moves along with the rhythms of its times, focusing the emotions, the suffering, the struggles, the dramas of those times. . . . The theatre must focus the total drama of contemporary life. A theatre of the past, nourished only by fantasies, is not theatre. It must arouse the emotions, like the classical theatre, that was the sensor of the heartbeat of its epoch. . . . (II, 982)

In these statements, drawn from interviews and a scant few public addresses, we have the only consistent expression of Lorca's ideas concerning the theatre. But in these observations, Lorca demonstrates his awareness of the problem of reception (both intellectual and emotional) as one of unique and far-reaching importance for an art form as immediate and intimate as theatre. The relationship between the spectator and the 'reality' being produced on the stage must be taken into account. The naturalistic theatre had set out to foster the illusion that what was presented on the stage was 'real', and that the actions of the feigned characters were authentic. The audience was to feel sympathetically in response to what they were seeing on the stage, and the dramatic action was to be understood by means of its accurate analogies with life outside the theatre. The stage was to be as nearly perfect an image of life as possible. And yet these effects had to be produced within a context of artificiality. The proscenium stage was like the ornate frame of a trompe l'oeil painting; the 'realism' was still a simulacrum, the product of a cleverly organised set of features designed to create an illusion.

To the degree that an ever more accurate resemblance to 'real life' and ever more accurate impersonations of 'real people' were sought on the naturalistic stage, the expressive range of the theatre was drastically reduced; that is, its quality as poetry and as an artistic medium with which Lorca was so concerned, was subordinated to its capacity to imitate the detail of everyday life outside. But to achieve the restoration of poetry to the stage, the playwright would first have to shake the audience out of its habitual expectation of verisimilitude. To do this, playwrights would need to take the initiative to confront the audience from the stage and in practice, and not merely in critical commentaries on the lamentable state of dramatic art.

In order to assault the illusion of reality and the familiarity upon which naturalism built its secure relationship to the public, playwrights had recourse to the worlds of fantasy (Lorca's *Butterfly's Evil Spell*; Maeterlinck; Yeats), the dream world, the surreal. The world of the stage moved farther away from a reality that was graspable, predictable, and susceptible to 'reasonable' (for the most part, socio-psychological) interpretation by its audiences. The rigorously constructed illusion of reality of the naturalistic stage was challenged by a stage world whose quality *as illusion* was its primary feature, and whose relationship to the experience of its public had to be sought on a level other than that of its resemblance to an objectively certified reality. Theatre called attention to its own artificiality and to its capacity to create something beyond a faithful series of images of a reality that was confidently claimed as its own by the audiences that applauded this mimetic enterprise. For example, Lorca openly seeks to establish this measure of artistic authority in his farces, where speakers in the prologues directly address the audience and turn their attention towards the territory that the play is staking out in the realm of the imagination. These prologues are essentially invitations to the spectators. The effort to break down resistance to the unreality of what the audience is about to see hinges on a kind of respectful mutual understanding between those in the audience and those on stage concerning the artificiality of the world they are about to experience on one side of the footlights, and to produce on the other. The prologues are also, certainly, little manifestos on theatre aesthetics and as such they have an educative aim as well. A theatre that could point to its own theatricality, and at the same time engage the audience in its play of imagination and its use of plain speech and poetry, music, movement and colour was a theatre that would have established the necessary authority to do so by successfully challenging the restraints of naturalism. Once this 'authority' was confirmed and acknowledged, then theatre would once again be able to move in the direction of exploring the broadest possible range of its own expressive qualities.

Authority, then, meant the integrity and the courage to address ethical, moral and social issues from the stage, and it also meant the power to challenge conventional ways of writing for the stage, of producing plays and of watching productions. Lorca's works are interrogations into both the ideological and the aesthetic qualities of theatre, and they are attempts to know to what extent these two aspects of authority were mutually dependent. What forms were necessary so that certain human problems and feelings could be most effectively treated on the stage? The ethical or ideological side of Lorca's preoccupation with the theatre was the one that dominated the conception and realisation of his major works written for the commercial stage: *Blood Wedding*, *Yerma*, *Doña Rosita the Spinster*, and the *House of Bernarda Alba*. The aesthetic problem of the dramatic illusion, and the phenomenological relationship between the audience and the theatrical production are most boldly confronted in his more 'difficult' works, works that call attention to themselves constantly as works of theatre and as concerted illusions: *As Soon as Five Years Go By*, *The Public*, and the posthumous fragment, 'Untitled Work'. Finally, it is in Lorca's full-length farce, *The Shoemaker's Wonderful Wife*, that we find the most surprising and transparent intersection of these two sides of the singular problem of authority in his theatre. In the farces and comedies this challenge to the imagination of the public and to the conventional forms of commercial theatre is most strikingly and engagingly made.

3
The Comic Theatre

Lorca undoubtedly began forming his impressions of comic theatre from a very early age, first as a spectator at the travelling puppet plays that came to his childhood home in Granada, then as a youthful imitator of these popular shows with family and friends as audiences, and continuing as he began to write his own theatrical works in Madrid. This popular theatre is important in all of Lorca's work for the stage. Guillermo de Torre, one of Lorca's friends from the early days in Granada, asserts that Lorca produced a number of farces based on the 'cristobitas', the Spanish guignol theatre (so-named after its most vivid stock figure, Don Cristóbal) and that these comic pieces were done even prior to his first drama written for performance in Madrid in 1920.[1] But these entertainments had no script and are therefore lost to us. In fact, all that remains from one of Lorca's earliest scripted puppet shows (1923) is a programme and a snap-shot of the stage. The performance took place on the occasion of the Feast of the Three Wise Men, 4 January 1923, before an audience of children and their parents in the parlour of the García home. In between a short opening work (entremés) by Cervantes with music by Stravinsky, and a medieval mystery play, *The Three Wisemen*, with original music by Lorca's co-producer, Manuel de Falla, there is listed a marionette play, *The Maiden Who Waters the Sweet Basil and the Inquisitive Prince*, authored by Lorca and based, he said, on a popular Andalusian folktale. Several noteworthy details are recollected by Francisco García Lorca, the poet's brother; the entire performance had musical accompaniment consisting of works by Albéñiz, Debussy and Ravel; between the acts of this puppet play, the traditional marionette figure, Don Cristóbal, appeared onstage manipulated by Lorca himself and entertained the audience with banter and dialogue.

Music was a constant presence in Lorca's life and would constitute an integral part of his work for the stage. Lorca was also fascinated by the implications of breaching the invisible wall that customarily separated the audience from the theatrical spectacle, whether that meant, as it did in the puppet farces, having a character from the drama address the public directly, or whether it involved a more complex interplay as in his later works. In 1934, eleven years after the Lorca–Falla chamber theatre production in Granada, the puppet Don Cristóbal again addressed an audience from the stage, only this time it was a sophisticated public in Buenos Aires, and he engaged in a dialogue with Lorca himself as a prelude to the performance of the *guignol*, *Don Cristóbal's Puppet Show*. Lorca was continually turning over in his mind a few monumental and characteristic themes, and a few very fundamental problems of dramatic form. In many ways, his work for the theatre, rather than being a succession of experiments with ever new themes and forms, is really a complex of persistent concerns that appear repeatedly in the most arrestingly new guises.

Federico García Lorca

**The Puppet Plays: 'The Tragicomedy of Don Cristóbal
and Mam'selle Rosita' (1928?) and 'Don Cristóbal's
Puppet Show' (1931)**

There is something about puppet theatre that is more
purely theatrical than live performance; perhaps it is the
absence of the mimetic pretence of live theatre that makes
possible in puppet theatre the magnification of dramatic
effects which in their turn take puppet theatre out of the
realm of the literary and into the realm of pure performance and dramatic action. When the actions or words of
human actors become mechanical, dehumanised or
'puppet-like', what is produced is a form of the grotesque.
When mechanical figures act in a human way the dramatic
image may be that of a starkly simplified caricature of
human behaviour and relationships which produces delight
in its graphic astuteness rather than revulsion in its
exaggeration. A kind of innocent illusion is thus set up that
plays directly on that pleasurable tension that is so fundamental to the theatrical experience between the drastic
artificiality of the representation and the reality to which it
alludes. And finally, puppet theatre was popular theatre,
and it represented to Lorca what he once described to
Manuel de Falla as, 'that exquisite popular feeling' (II,
1118). Lorca later put the following words in the mouth of
the Director' who addresses the audience at the beginning
of *Don Cristóbal's Puppet Show*: 'Puppet theatre is the
expression of the imagination of the people, and it brings
forth that feeling of their popular grace and innocence' (II,
491).

   The two puppet plays, *The Tragicomedy of Don Cristóbal and Mam'selle Rosita* and *Don Cristóbal's Puppet
Show* are both farces, and the *Puppet Show* seems to be a
carefully revised version of the earlier *Tragicomedy*. The

40

latter play calls for a cast of well over twenty characters while *Puppet Show* calls for seven. Except for the lyrics of the songs, *Tragicomedy* is in prose, while in *Puppet Show*, verse and prose alternate throughout. Finally, there is some doubt as to whether the *Tragicomedy* was really intended as a puppet play at all, or whether Lorca may have intended it as that originally and ended up writing a work that is really more suited for a full-scale stage production. When Lorca mentioned his plans for performances of the *Tragicomedy* sometimes it was for actors and actresses, and as late as 1935 he was projecting its performance with marionettes.[2] As for *Don Cristóbal's Puppet Show*, there is little question but that Lorca's revisions were carried out with an eye to making this later version of the Don Cristóbal and Señorita Rosita story one that would be exclusively for puppets and one that would display all of Lorca's skills and sensitivity in drawing together the essential qualities of this genre of folk theatre in an original creation.

The dramatic action of the two plays moves along the same conventional lines. The young and beautiful Doña Rosita is being forced by a parent (in one play, the mother, in the other the father) to marry the brutal and repugnant but wealthy Don Cristóbal. Doña Rosita, however, already has a lover whose continued presence poses a challenge to Don Cristóbal's hold on her, and consequently, a threat to his masculine honour. The *Tragicomedy* is built around a much greater variety of scenes and of dramatic action than the *Puppet Show*, and the competition for Doña Rosita's love is drawn out to a far greater extent. The final scene of the play is the standard one from bedroom farce where each contender for Rosita's affection visits her in her room and must hide as the next one arrives. The two suitors pop in and out of separate wardrobe closets and wail their frustration as Don Cristóbal marries Doña Rosita and they prepare for their nuptial night. The final scene is one of great confusion and frantic action, with Rosita opening and closing closet doors, her lovers emerging, one to be chased and beaten by Don Cristóbal, the other hugging and kissing Doña Rosita all the while. The climax is also in the tradition of classic farce as the lascivious old man is defeated and removed from the scene entirely. Don Cristóbal literally bursts from rage and collapses in a heap with the sound of breaking springs. When he is removed from the stage, he produces a wheezing and moaning sound like a bagpipe. The young lovers thus discover that Cristóbal was not even a 'real person', and they celebrate their love and their triumph over him to end the play.

The movement of the later and shorter *Don Cristóbal's Puppet Show* is much more rapid and schematic in comparison to the *Tragicomedy*. Here, Cristóbal starts out needing to acquire the wealth to marry Doña Rosita and the Director tells him to go out and get it. In the first scene, Cristóbal takes the role of the traditional *guignol* quack doctor who, by way of treatment, submits his unhappy patient to such a drubbing with his club that he kills him, then steals all his money and throws him off the stage. Cristóbal becomes wealthy in this play before our very eyes. In the *Puppet Show*, Doña Rosita is a ripe young thing, full of erotic ardour, whose mother sells her off to Don Cristóbal by graphically extolling her sexual attractions. Rosita seems compliant and willing to marry anyone.

All the characters are terrified of Cristóbal's temper and his lethal club, but on their wedding night, when he dozes off, one character after the other (including the 'patient' Cristóbal earlier killed) darts on to the stage to kiss Rosita, and they dart off again immediately when Don Cristóbal wakes up. Rosita then complains of a belly-ache, goes off into the wings and quickly gives birth to four babies, sending Don Cristóbal into a fit of jealous rage. Her mother insists the babies are Cristóbal's, he beats her senseless for her trouble and throws her off the stage. He then grabs Rosita and begins to beat her as the play ends abruptly with the intervention of the narrator-director.

The dialogue in *Puppet Show* is so rapid as to have the very effect of action; the pace of the action is typically frenetic. In this shorter play as well, the dialogue is more often an exchange of rhyming verse whose comic effect is achieved, not from what is said, but from how it is said and how outrageous, ribald and often obscene the level of expression can be.

In contrast, the *Tragicomedy*'s scenes are far more elaborately framed and the dialogue is full of nuances which, along with the conventional action, could success-fully be played as broad farce by actors and actresses. The speeches here are for the most part more substantial than in the *Puppet Show*, and they serve in many instances to elaborate a character's feelings, especially Rosita's, who in this play is a comic-pathetic victim of her father's and Don Cristóbal's plotting. The pace does not reach the rapidity demanded by traditional farce until the final scene, whereas that pace is sustained throughout *Don Cristóbal's Puppet Show*.

In both these plays, even with the fidelity to highly conventional forms of action and speech that Lorca attains, there is a sly sophistication, a dramatic self-consciousness and a characteristic tendency to refer consistently to their own artificiality as stage works.

The *Tragicomedy* opens with an address to the audience delivered by a Mosquito, a 'mysterious character, half fairy, half sprite, half insect', who is to represent, according to the author's indications, the 'joy of the free life, and the good humour [*gracia*] and poetry of the Andalucian people' (II, 61). The Mosquito (and here we must not rule out the possibility of a bit of self-parody on Lorca's part after his disastrous insect play) speaks directly to the audience, declaring that he and his company are refugees, fleeing from the commercial theatres where they have been locked away from view. El Mosquito invites the audience to join with these traditional *guignol* characters (whether actors or puppets is never specified) in a liberating escapade, away from the soporific theatre of the urban bourgeoisie, out to the open fields and into the innocent and extravagant world of the popular farce. The tone of Mosquito's remarks is exuberant, and the style suggestive and lyrical. Three more times during the play Mosquito will enter to comment on the situation to the audience, and twice to annoy sleeping characters on stage. He finally appears to sing the song of victory over the vanquished Don Cristobita. Mosquito thus sustains his initial role as the all-knowing spirit; he is a Puck-like figure, both in the drama as a character, and out of it as he addresses the public. He thereby sustains the entire play at a level of fanciful illusion and comic artifice.

The prologue to the *Puppet Show*, on the other hand, takes the audience directly to a problem concerning the aesthetics of this popular genre and its proper place as a form of theatre. The audience witnesses an important struggle that goes on between the Poet who has written the work, and the Director who is in charge of its production. The audience is alerted to the 'delicious' and profane language that is characteristic of the popular puppet theatre, and the Director hopes that it will not affront their cultivated sensibilities.

The Poet is then allowed to address a few words to the audience, and after cajoling them into silence, he reveals himself to be a thoroughly subversive individual. For in spite of the fact that he works like a servant under the Director, writing scripts as well as ironing costumes for the company backstage, he is anxious for the audience to know that he is possession of some secret knowledge about the world that he seems to be on the verge of telling us. When he goes on to make a claim to have some secret insight as well into the character of Don Cristóbal, whom we are about to see in this play, the Director will tolerate no more:

DIRECTOR: You, as a poet, have no right to reveal the secrets that underlie all our lives.

POET: Yes sir.

DIRECTOR: Don't I pay you your wages?

POET: Yes sir, But it's just that Don Cristóbal, I know that deep down he is a good person, and that he could perhaps come to behave that way.

DIRECTOR: You charlatan. If you don't shut up I'll come out there and break that flour-paste face of yours. Who are you to do away with the law of evil? (II, 492)

And as if this were not enough, the Director then forces the Poet publicly to recant his heresy, and to reaffirm the dogma:

DIRECTOR: Say what you have to say and what the public knows to be the truth.

POET: Respectable public: as a poet, I must tell you that Don Cristóbal is evil.

DIRECTOR: And he cannot be good.

POET: And he cannot be good.

DIRECTOR: More. Go on.

POET: I'm going on, Señor Director. And he never will be able to be good.

DIRECTOR: Very nice. How much do I owe you? (II, 493)

This amounts to a very subtle and important exchange on the aesthetics of realism in the theatre, and on the sensibilities of the theatre audience in general. In the first place, the public has already been enticed and charmed by the Director and the Poet alike into going along with this flight away from the suffocating world of the bourgeoise drama and into the liberating atmosphere of this most venerable form of folk theatre. The suggestion of the impertinent Poet, however, is that the folk characters we are about to see are really inflexible stereotypes whose behaviour has been rigidly determined by a sort of tyranny of dramatic tradition. Advocating a profounder and more challenging vision of character, the Poet wishes to break with the tradition that has limited the way in which the stock figures of the *guignol* may be portrayed. During a subsequent interruption of the play, the Poet even suggests that the characters themselves have had enough of this rigidity, 'Because Don Cristóbal is not that way, nor is Doña Rosita . . . I mean, they're getting tired of this' (II, 507).

Over the course of this debate, Lorca lures the audience into a position of solidarity with the Poet and with other dramatists like him who would attack the hackneyed theatrical stereotypes of the past in the name of a renewed complexity of character portrayal. The Poet makes his point, and it is of fundamental importance to the future of the theatre, but he seems to have chosen entirely the wrong battleground. There are values operating in the guignol theatre that have little to do with psychological realism and Lorca was determined to bring those values as well directly before the public of his day. Specifically, Lorca wished to illustrate the idea of the theatre as *play*, both physical and verbal, where the dramatic medium – puppets – is so thoroughly artificial that the pleasure derived by the spectator is based predominantly in the performance, in the illusion and the fantasy of the spectacle, and not in its mimetic qualities or its verisimilitude.

But why has Lorca brought this little debate between the values of the puppet farce (enforced tyrannically by the Director) and the values of more serious drama (defended unsuccessfully by the Poet) into this particular play that seems to have been so carefully crafted in order to capture in its purest form the popular flavour of its folk origins? For Lorca, the fullest potential of theatre would be realised when the most thorough synthesis of these two currents in the history of European drama was achieved. As late as 1934, Lorca performed the *Puppet Show* before a sophisticated audience in Buenos Aires, and he engaged the puppet Don Cristóbal himself in a preliminary dialogue on stage before the curtain went up. In their conversation they agree upon the need for this uninhibited and popular form of theatre to be brought out of the obscurity in which it has languished. 'You are a mainstay of the theatre, Don Cristóbal,' Lorca declares, 'all theatre descends from you' (I, 1174). And if he decided to bring this theatre before cultivated audiences in its purest and most boisterous form, then it is specifically because of the need Lorca saw to attack in the most startling and captivating way he could the insipid and soporific commercial theatre of his day. The earlier and more lengthy *Tragicomedy of Don Cristóbal and Mam'selle Rosita* was a liberal poetic elaboration of a conventional puppet drama that lost much of the spontaneity and ribaldry of its popular models in the more theatrical qualities it acquired. *Don Cristóbal's Puppet Show*, on the other hand, is a carefully-wrought and even self-conscious (to the extent that the project is debated in the course of the work itself) return to the original form of the folk theatre for marionettes. Lorca had these models still close at hand when he wrote the more ambitious and synthetic *Shoemaker's Wonderful Wife*, where the synthesis he had hinted at in the prologue to *Puppet Show* between conventional comic forms and complex portrayal of character is most perfectly achieved.

'The Shoemaker's Wonderful Wife' (1933)

This play occupied Lorca off and on for many years. In a letter to a friend from 1923 (II, 1065), we learn that he had completed the first act of a comedy that he said was in the style of the *Cristobitas* – the Spanish Punch and Judy shows – that were the inspiration for his *Tragicomedy* and for the *Puppet Show*. Later, in the introductory remarks he published for the 1933 performance of *The Shoemaker's Wonderful Wife* in Buenos Aires, Lorca stated that he had written the play in the summer of 1926, characterising the project almost as a personal response to *avant-garde* movements in European art in general:

> The troubled letters I was getting from my friends in Paris during their beautiful and bitter struggle with abstract art led me to write, by way of reaction, this almost vulgar fable, with its direct version of reality, wherein I wanted to weave an invisible thread of poetry, but where the comic gesture and the humour would stand out clear and undisguised at the surface.[3]

In the winter of 1929–30, during his stay in New York City, Lorca was probably working again on the play, and about a year later, in December 1930, it had its debut on the Madrid stage. The version performed, however, was shorter (a 'chamber version', Lorca called it) than the one upon which the best-known translation is based.[4] The definitive play was performed in Buenos Aires in November of 1933, and subsequently in Madrid in March of 1935, with the addition of songs and dances, and with expanded lyrics. *The Shoemaker's Wonderful Wife* was a serious project, and one that matured along with Lorca's own maturity as a writer. When he first began the play, he was working along the lines of the traditional Spanish farce for puppets. By the time the play found its definitive version, some ten years later, Lorca had assimilated into this comic work a wealth of Spanish popular and literary tradition, from the origins of the story in the ballads of the unhappy young wife, married to the old man, through the 'interludes' of Cervantes and the brilliantly theatrical verse drama of the Spanish Golden Age. The play is now a sophisticated and complex work with a highly personal and characteristic poetic theme, but one which at the same time consciously displays its heritage in the popular as well as the classical Spanish stage.

Lorca opens the *Shoemaker's Wonderful Wife* with a prologue directed to the audience, in this case to be delivered by the Author himself. The Author begins by stating his refusal either to speak obsequiously or to beg the indulgence of his public. Poetry and imagination, he declares, have been banished from the theatre due to the fear that poets have of not pleasing paying audiences. But the Author proclaims that he has long since broken through that barrier of intimidation that separates the poet from the public. At the same time, however, he promises that he will not tax his audience's credulity in this play by presenting astonishing miracles on the stage. Instead, he says, the return of poetry to the theatre is to be accomplished through the particular example set forth in this play, suggesting that the Shoemaker's Wife will embody the poetic spirit that the Author is talking about, and that the play will in and of itself exemplify how poetry can properly be played before a theatre audience. As if to emphasise comically that no matter what, the stage is always a world of illusion, the poet, while he finishes addressing the audience also must contend with the Shoemaker's Wife – or the actress playing her part – who is demanding loudly that she be allowed immediately to make her entrance onstage. The Author is now at the same time part of the stage world, and part of the world of the spectators listening to the Shoemaker's Wife shouting from the wings.

Finally, to embellish even more this back-and-forth play between illusion and the world of the audience, the Author calls for the Shoemaker's Wife to come onstage, and he tips his hat in farewell; the hat begins to glow with a green light from within and a stream of water pours out of it on to the floor. This is the most tangible warning to the audience that the most unexpected and extraordinary things can happen on the stage. But the small miracle of the Shoemaker's Wife's poetic soul, while altogether less spectacular and artificial than the Author's trick hat, is to be every bit as marvellous. Some kinds of magic in the theatre can amaze the public like the work of a clever sleight-of-hand artist; but, Lorca suggests, there is a different kind of magic to be experienced as well, a kind more properly identified with poetry.

Lorca's *Tragicomedy* ends with the youthful bride and her lover united in triumph over the enraged and foolish old Don Cristóbal. The *Puppet Show* ends with the dishonoured husband, Cristóbal, beating both his mother-in-law and his wife after she has given birth to four illegitimate babies. The *Shoemaker's Wonderful Wife* retains the old husband and the young bride, but here it is the mild-mannered husband who has reluctantly given in to the nagging of his sister and married the beautiful but needy young girl, and it is the new bride who dominates the household. If at first the young wife's fits of temper seem to spring from her frustration with the bland and unpromising marriage she has made, we soon discover that there is something in her character that interests us beyond the hyperbolic comedy of her outbursts against her hapless husband. Lorca has begun with the standard formula for farce and introduced into it a vivid and original representation of the traditional shrewish wife with her beleaguered husband. He has given her character an unexpected dimension that is the particular genius and the ultimate importance of this play. The Shoemaker's Wife is the embodiment of the poetic spirit that fluctuates dramatically between a state of lyric rapture in the ideal world of her imagination, and a state of wild despair over the mediocrity of the reality she finds herself facing every day. Lorca described very clearly the complexity he wished to achieve in his creation of the Wife's character:

> [The play] is a simple farce, of a purely classical tone wherein is depicted the spirit of a woman who is just like all other women, and who becomes at the same time, and in a gentle way, an apology for the human soul. Thus it is, then, that the Shoemaker's Wife is at once a type and an archetype; she is a fundamental [*primaria*] creature and a myth of our own pure and unsatisfied idealism.[5]

When Lorca declared that poetry had to be restored to its rightful place on the stage he certainly had in mind a theatre whose performance would seek to achieve a heightened emotional and sensory experience for its audiences through the fullest use of the characteristic resources of the medium, such as stage design, music, costume, dance and the expressive capacities of the human voice and body. At the same time, in its representation of the human character, *The Shoemaker's Wonderful Wife* projects the idea of just what the poetic spirit is like, and suggests that it is a dimension of the individual that is universally shared. The Shoemaker's Wife's constant recourse to her world of fantasy is one of Lorca's most compelling examples of this capacity of the spirit to create imaginatively an ideal world to replace a real one that by definition can never completely satisfy.

As the play begins, the Wife is loudly defending herself against the criticism of her neighbours as she comes in from the street. She then turns to her pusillanimous husband who is busily mending shoes and begins to berate him and to lament the fate that brought her to marry him. She does everything a wife should do around the house, but, as she says, she will never be her husband's slave, and she will otherwise do exactly as she pleases. The mayor of the town then drops in for a visit, casting lascivious looks at the young bride while instructing her meek husband in the proper way to handle spirited women and warning him to look after his own honour. The Wife is later visited by no less than three young suitors, all of whom are seeking her affection, and she angrily sends them all away. But her husband has heeded and believes the public gossip about his wife's alleged loose conduct, and, in desperation, he abandons her as the first act ends.

The second act opens to find the Wife earning her living in her husband's absence by operating a tavern. When she thinks of her husband, she remembers him as he certainly never was: dashing and handsome, wearing a cape and mounted on a splendid horse. The sinister mayor and the other young swains are still trying to attract her attention but she has steadfastly spurned all their enticements.

Soon the Shoemaker himself returns home, disguised as

a puppet master, and he sets up his theatre in the Wife's tavern. He then presents a little play to his wife and the neighbours who gather there, and the plot turns out to be analogous to his own situation with his wife, except that in the play the bride has a lover, and together they plot the death of the aged husband. Before the Shoemaker's drama can end, however, a knife fight breaks out in the street between two of the Wife's suitors, and when all rush out to see, the Puppeteer/Shoemaker and his wife are left alone. Now the Shoemaker tests his wife's reaction to the dramatised story she has just seen, and he hears her say that she has been faithful, that she still loves her husband, and that she condemns the treachery of the lovers in the play. Still unrecognised by his wife, the Shoemaker tells her about his own domineering wife who constantly 'dreamed of a world that was not mine', and soon ran away from home. The Wife, encouraged by this frank exchange, describes her fugitive husband who has now been transformed through the fantasy of her memory: '. . . in spite of his fifty and some odd years, his most blessed fifty years, I find him more slender and graceful than all the men in the world.'[6] The Shoemaker then confesses that he would now be happy to let his wife 'command the castle' if only she would come back and be forgiven; she confesses her undying love for her husband, and her wish to forgive him if only he will return home. The skilfully delayed moment of reconciliation is at hand and the Shoemaker joyfully tears off his disguise. His wife is both horrified and overjoyed as the absolute contradiction of her situation is most dramatically revealed to her in all its force. She therefore assails her husband with a mixture of abuse and expressions of delight at his return. Finally, and most importantly, they stand inside their house, united as never before against their petty neighbours who come to taunt the Wife with their songs. 'Loafer, scoundrel, rascal, villain! Do you hear that? [referring to the mocking crowd outside]. All because of you!' she shrieks at her husband; and then, 'Oh how happy I am you've returned!' and finally, 'Oh how unfortunate I am! With the man God has given to me! . . . There are two of us now, two! Two! My husband and I. . . . Oh, this scoundrel, oh this villain!' (*5 Plays*, 104).

Although this reconciliation of sorts would seem to point to a circular structure for the plot of this play, the ending does not actually represent a return to the situation at the beginning of the drama. The Shoemaker has obtained the tangible proof he needs of the integrity and devotion of his wife, and he will now join with her to defend their home against the vulgar calumny of the mob outside. And she, confronted once again with the mediocrity and the utter unalterability of her domestic situation, will continue to embellish her own and her husband's life as well with her priceless gift of poetic imagination. The relationship at the end, therefore, is an entirely new one, and it has been forged out of the necessity to unite these two disparate personalities in opposition to an ignorant world outside that has disdained them both. The Shoemaker, who formerly represented the passive acceptance of the 'real' world, has been moved to take action; he leaves home rather than suffer the scorn of the community and the tyranny of his wife. He also assumes a new role, that of the puppeteer or the poet-dramatist, and thereby discovers for himself the truth about his wife by means of creating a dramatic illusion, a kind of test-reality by which to gauge his wife's feelings. His puppet show, by presenting a plausible but fantastic version of the deceit that he feared his wife was engaged in, is a clear example – introduced by Lorca within his own play – of the resonances that art can have in the everyday reality of those who experience it. The

Shoemaker's Wife, on the other hand, already knows about the necessity and the value of poetic illusion. It is her susceptibility to it, in fact, that has allowed the play within the play to have its profound effect. To see his wife sobbing as the lovers in the puppet play plot the murder of the decent old husband is all the Shoemaker needs to open his eyes to the real character of his young bride. She will of course continue her tireless struggle against the passive acceptance of the mediocre and the 'real', never satisfied with what she can touch or attain. Her world of poetic imagination is the way in which she achieves her independence and maintains her own integrity.

In *Don Cristóbal's Puppet Show* the Poet and the Director argue about the possible complexities of a stock character such as Don Cristóbal. If the discovery of such complexities is impossible in a play where Lorca wished to maintain fidelity to his popular model, then *The Shoemaker's Wonderful Wife* is the way in which those complexities are brilliantly revealed, even as the spontaneity and the theatrical qualities of the traditional farce are preserved. In other words, if, as the Poet asserts in the *Puppet Show*, Don Cristóbal is not necessarily evil, then the Shoemaker's Wife is not necessarily the conventional figure of comic farce: the frustrated and seductive child bride and the cuckholder of her senile husband. She is none of these things, although admittedly she exhibits manifold qualities of that stereotypical comic role. Lorca allows us to enjoy the world of the classic farce to its fullest, while at the same time demonstrating the possibilities for poetically developing a complex characterisation of the human spirit. The audience is thus drawn into a festive solidarity with the triumphs of the Wife's spirit, and with the theatrical values that her character and the play itself represent. This is the true and unexpected 'wonder' of this unassuming comedy that the Author ironically and mysteriously prepares us for in his prologue to the audience.

Lorca said that in the *Shoemaker's Wonderful Wife* he had worked to attain a rhythm that would be lively and flowing throughout the play, and that he had used music, as he put it, to '*desrealizar la escena*' – that is, to undermine the naturalistic effect of the dramatic illusion and to make it seem, literally, 'unreal'. In terms of the dramatic experience itself, he specifically wished to 'eliminate from people's minds the idea that "this is really happening", and to enhance the poetic dimensions [of the play] with the same purposes as our classical authors did' (I, 1143). Invoking the theatre of Lope de Vega, Tirso de Molina and Calderón de la Barca as sources of his inspiration, Lorca implies here that he is not doing anything particularly new or revolutionary by bringing poetry and music to the stage, except in so far as the canons of realism had determined since the mid-nineteenth century that speech was to be in prose and ought to be a plausible representation of 'real' speech, and that dramatic activity should also approximate 'real' activity and seem 'natural' to the audience that had become accustomed to viewing a familiar world on the stage. In order to move audiences beyond these habitual expectations, Lorca knew that he would have to marshal all the theatre's historic resources and find his models in historic periods when the theatre had been characterised by its very theatricality, its artificiality and its distinctness from 'natural' activity. It was Lorca's conviction that the public's emotional and intellectual experience of drama would be intensified and deepened as the human and material resources brought to bear on the conception and production of plays were expanded and enriched. Imaginative costuming and choreography would extend the expressive range of the human body in the theatre, and poetry and singing would enhance the communicative powers of the voice and speech.

'The Love of Don Perlimplín and Belisa in the Garden' (1933)

Although this play is only what Lorca called a sketch or a 'salon version' of what was to become a more substantial work, it stands as an indication of what Lorca wished to accomplish in this effort to create a greatly heightened theatrical experience. The play is also the most daring of the comic pieces in its experimentation with tone. While it depends upon traditional models for its characters and plot, Lorca did not intend to write just another farce. In 1924 he characterised the work as 'a grotesque play' (II, 1078), and in 1933, on the eve of the opening of a programme including *The Shoemaker's Wonderful Wife*, and *Don Perlimplín*, Lorca declared, 'what I have been interested in doing in *Don Perlimplín* is to highlight the contrast between the lyric and the grotesque and even to mix them at every turn' (II, 908). In contrast to the festive tone of the *Shoemaker's Wonderful Wife*, *Don Perlimplín* begins as a farce, but very quickly an undertone of pathos emerges and the combination is far more disquieting than humorous in the end. It is as though the conventional theme of the cuckolded old man were being subjected to the kind of scrutiny that would discover the real complexity of the sexual theme that had always remained innocently hidden beneath the surface of the comic action. In other ways too, such as in his introduction of fantastic creatures – the sprites in scene one – and in his purely symbolic use of the stage set, also in the first scene, Lorca carried this particular theme still farther away from its popular origins.

In the prologue, the arrangements for the marriage of

Don Perlimplín to Belisa are made. Like the Shoemaker, Don Perlimplín is a bachelor of over fifty years of age who has lived under the protection and care of a mother-figure – in this case, his maid, Marcolfa. Don Perlimplín is wealthy, and the union is eagerly agreed to by Belisa's mother who, like the mother in the farcical *Puppet Show*, broadly hints at the sexual delights her daughter has to offer. Don Perlimplín, however, is a sexual adolescent, a virgin, frightened of women, but awakening slowly to his first encounter as he listens to Belisa's erotic song coming from her balcony window:

> Ah love, ah love.
> Tight in my warm thighs imprisoned
> There swims like a fish the sun.
> Warm water in the rushes.
> Ah love.   (*5 Plays*, 108)

A flock of black paper birds that crosses the open balcony before the curtain falls, however, portends the change of tone that soon emerges.

Scene one introduces the newlyweds on their nuptial night in their bedroom. Belisa is an exaggerated stereotype of sensuality who, when she hears the serenade of guitars from outside, says, 'Whoever seeks me ardently will find me. My thirst is never quenched. . . .' (*5 Plays*, 113) For his part, Don Perlimplín confesses to her that he did not love her when they married, but when he watched her dressing through the keyhole, he 'felt love come to me, then!' (*5 Plays*, 114). As the couple turn out the bedroom light, a curtain is discreetly drawn over the scene by two sprites who then face the audience and mischievously discuss their role in the drama:

2ND SPRITE: It's always nice to cover other people's failings. . . .

1ST SPRITE: And then to let the audience take care of uncovering them.

2ND SPRITE: Because if things are not covered up with all possible precautions. . . .

1ST SPRITE: They would never be discovered.

2ND SPRITE: And without this covering and uncovering . . .

1ST SPRITE: What would the poor people do?

(5 Plays, 115)

The audience is now alerted that there will be something extraordinary to apprehend in this play, and that it will not be at the surface of what they see and hear. As if to underscore their words, the curtains are pulled back and we see the beginning of the drama's symbolic discourse as Don Perlimplín is sitting on the bed wearing a huge pair of golden horns decorated with flowers. In the room there are six doors, five of them leading to exterior balconies, and all five are open with sunlight streaming in. Five men's hats are seen on the bedroom floor. Don Perlimplín is in a rapture after his night with Belisa (his first ever with a woman), but as she goes back to sleep, he sings a song whose imagery of love and mutilation is a grim foreshadowing.

Scene two sets the stage for the intrigue that is to develop at the end of the play: Belisa is being courted by a mysterious young man, and Don Perlimplín's role is changing radically before our eyes. In contrast to the old man who is the obstacle to his young bride's sexual liaisons, Don Perlimplín is seen here as the advocate and facilitator of Belisa's extramarital affair. Don Perlimplín's interest in this lover is intense. Belisa reads aloud to him one of the suitor's letters that speaks to her about her erotic attractiveness. Don Perlimplín then announces that he, the old husband, far from standing in the way, wants to sacrifice himself for Belisa's happiness. He has become abstracted from the 'world or morals' that would condemn his actions and ridicule him as a cuckold. With his grandiose exit, he announces cryptically that Belisa will soon know all the truth.

In scene three, Don Perlimplín attempts enigmatically to explain to Marcolfa the reasons for his behaviour. He has succeeded in having Belisa fall hopelessly in love with the youth who wrote the seductive letter, though she has never spoken to him. When Marcolfa expresses her horror at his encouragement of this illicit and immoral affair, and asks how he can possibly do it, Perlimplín exclaims, 'Because Perlimplín has no honor and wants to avenge himself! Now do you see?' (*5 Plays*, 125). Of course Marcolfa does not see at this point, and for that matter, neither does the audience. But the fact is that this 'amusement' – and it turns out to be the most serious of undertakings – involves the contrivance of an illusion by Perlimplín. Just as the Shoemaker used the power of theatre to reach his wife's conscience, so Perlimplín organises 'reality' in such a way that his wife falls irrevocably in love with a stranger who does not exist. Belisa goes into the garden by night to await a rendezvous with her mysterious lover. Perlimplín 'discovers' her there and she confesses that she loves this youth more now than ever before. Perlimplín announces mysteriously that this love affair represents the triumph of *his* imagination, saying that, since Belisa loves this man so much, and in order that he may be completely hers and never leave her, he, Perlimplín, will kill the suitor with his dagger. 'He will love you with the infinite love of the dead,' Perlimplín declares (*5 Plays*, 128). Upon which he leaves, and a moment later a figure wrapped in a red cape staggers on to the stage. The presumed lover cries out that Belisa's husband has killed him, but when the cape is drawn aside, Belisa discovers that the stranger is Perlimplín himself, and that he has plunged his knife into his own heart. Belisa's lover has been Perlimplín's invention; the erotic letters, the rendezvous, and most importantly the passion they have aroused in Belisa, all represent in fact the triumph of Perlimplín's imagination. We recall Perlimplín's words to Belisa at the end of the second scene: 'Since I am an old man, I want to sacrifice myself for you. This that I do no one ever did before. But I am already beyond the world and the ridiculous morals of its people. Good-by. . . . Later you will know everything. Later' (*5 Plays*, 123). So Perlimplín, split into two separate persons – the old husband, and the young lover – has murdered Belisa's apochryphal lover by committing suicide.

Perhaps owing to the fact that this version of the play was seen by Lorca as preliminary to a longer drama where the theme would be developed in all its complexity, the movement of the action from farce to grotesque pathos seems quite precipitous. The Prologue where the bargaining for the marriage goes on has all the rapid pace and verbal play that characterise the play's comedic forerunners, but from the opening of the first scene to the suicide at the end of the play, this lighter tone is quickly replaced by complexities of action and of symbolic discourse that are accompanied by a deliberate series of distortions and skewed perspectives in the stage design. The overwhelming erotic presence of Belisa on the wedding night makes the virginal old man beside her seem infantile, and she teases him as though he were a child. This contradictory scene, which should be comic, is instead disconcerting owing to the strangeness of the exaggerated costumes and the mysterious whistles that presage the appearance of the sprites. The sprites talk of dark secrets and then reveal the horned Perlimplín and the evidence that Belisa's charms are sought after by more than just her new husband. Scene two calls for the perspectives in Perlimplín's dining room to be 'deliciously wrong', and for the objects on the table to be painted 'as in a primitive Last Supper'. Belisa's costume is wildly extravagant: '*a red dress of eighteenth-century style. The skirt at the back is slit, allowing stockings to be seen. She wears huge earrings and a red hat trimmed with big ostrich feathers*' (*5 Plays*, 120). The scene ends with Perlimplín's enigmatic announcement of his intention to sacrifice himself. By now there is an overtone of madness in Perlimplín's behaviour: he is obsessed by his secret plan, and he is almost euphoric as he anticipates its results. The final discovery of Perlimplín's charade and the violence he directs against himself constitute the last step in Lorca's merging of the comic, the pathetic and the grotesque.

Is there a nobility in Perlimplín's sacrificial murder/suicide? In his disguise as the dying youth, he declares that Belisa's husband, as he struck with his dagger, had shouted, 'Belisa has a soul!' (*5 Plays*, 129). The object of Belisa's arousal (the fantasy lover) is removed in the same bloody act that annihilates Perlimplín, who has 'written the script' for this dramatic hoax. And it happens at the precise dramatic moment when Belisa has been carefully prepared to anticipate the physical satisfaction of her desire for the Young Man. Her trauma and bewilderment at the end are profound. Can it be that her very anguish over the complex enigma of this final act is what Perlimplín means by having a soul? Or is Perlimplín motivated by a noble desire to cause Belisa to transcend her lasciviousness and attain a more sublime level of platonic devotion where there is no hope of reciprocation or satisfaction because love's object is an impossibility? Or does he contrive this bit of theatre consciously or unconsciously as the ultimate revenge of an old man who has been incapable of satisfying a creature whose sexual appetite constitutes a nightmare of torment for him? Is it not the most perverse of torments to have aroused Belisa to an erotic encounter only to present her with the horror of a bloody suicide? In spite of the attractiveness of finding an altruistic motive in Perlimplín's 'sacrifice' (the most common interpretation among Lorca critics), there is compelling evidence that points to a darker and more distorted psychological motive behind this shocking act.[7] The symbolic nature of the play supports the simultaneous existence of both these levels of motivation. In Lorca's own conception, after all, the play was a fusion of both the lyric and the grotesque, and this complexity of tone can then certainly be seen as the effective analogue to the complexity of interpretation that is necessary here.

These plays occupied Lorca off and on for fifteen years – that is, throughout his entire career as a dramatist and poet. Although none of them is of sufficient length to occupy a programme by itself, each one displays important aspects of Lorca's dramatic art. What is perhaps most striking is the range of possibilities for the stage that is explored from one of these works to the next. Even Lorca's early misadventure with lyrical symbolism in the *Butterfly's Evil Spell* was, after all, not a complete loss when we can observe that elements such as the close integration of programme music, dance and song with a dramatic text came to constitute major aspects of the production values of the *Shoemaker's Wonderful Wife* and *Don Perlimplín*. Moreover, the prologues to the *Tragicomedy*, *Don Cristóbal's Puppet Show* and *The Shoemaker's Wonderful Wife* not only constitute valuable insights into the aesthetics of the theatre that

Lorca wished to bring directly to the attention of the public, but they are themselves ingenious plays back and forth between the illusory reality of the stage world and the 'other reality' of the spectator.

4
The Granada Plays

In both *Mariana Pineda* and *Doña Rosita the Spinster*
Granada is the setting, but it is not a Granada that Lorca
knew first-hand. Lorca evokes an atmosphere of the past,
and in these two plays the past serves at once as an
historical context for the dramatic action, and as a kind of
homage on Lorca's part to theatre of the past and to past
aesthetic sensibilities that still had considerable currency in
the Granada, and even the Spain that Lorca knew as a
young man. The world of romantic verse drama is recalled
in Lorca's conception of *Mariana Pineda*; in the melancholy provincialism of *Doña Rosita the Spinster* the precious aesthetic of late nineteenth-century popularised mod-
ernism permeates the atmosphere, while a kind of Chekho-
vian poetic realism defines the play's form and style.

Although separated in their appearance on the stage by
some eight years, what unites these two works is that they
were both conceived as poetic evocations of a specific time
and place, and as representations of the intimate drama of
their respective female protagonists. To this end, Lorca set

about exploring the resources of the theatre itself as a means to this evocation, and the eight years that intervene between the production of these two works simply indicate the persistent and searching nature of that exploration. Both plays were initially inspired as projects in Lorca's imagination within a year of one another, *Mariana Pineda* being written between 1923 and 1925, and the idea for *Doña Rosita* being suggested to Lorca in 1924. The first work was written and produced soon after Lorca conceived the idea, and it was to some extent at least, motivated by the need that Lorca felt to vindicate himself as a writer of drama after his first work had failed on the stage of the Teatro Eslava. In contrast, Lorca said that the later play was completed in his mind as soon as the idea was suggested to him by a friend's reading of a certain passage from a book on flowers, but that he had delayed its formal composition until 1935: 'It came to me in finished form, impossible to revise. And, nevertheless, I did not write it down until 1935. The years have embroidered the scenes and have put poetry to the story of the flower.'[1] Those intervening years had given Lorca the necessary control over his artistic medium to make *Doña Rosita* one of his most subtle and successful works for the stage.

'Mariana Pineda' (1927)

The story that Lorca elaborates in this drama takes place in Granada about 1830. Lorca subtitles his play, 'a popular ballad in three lithographs', giving an indication thereby of the antique and somewhat remote quality he wishes to impart. The Bourbon monarch, Fernando VII, restored to the Spanish throne after the Napoleonic interlude, was waging a war of relentless terror and repression against the liberal and constitutionalist movements that had flourished in the country after the victorious struggle to expel Joseph Bonaparte and the occupying French armies. To avoid persecution, the opposition movements had become clandestine, often relying on the collaboration of those who were sympathetic to their cause, but who could also still move about freely in society. Mariana Pineda, a young widow and mother of two, conspired with the liberal movement in Granada, was trapped and imprisoned by the local authorities, who used as evidence against her the fact that she had embroidered a banner for the rebels. After refusing to reveal the names of any co-conspirators, she was tried and executed in 1831. Lorca's dramatic rendering of Mariana Pineda's story introduces a love affair between Mariana and one of the clandestine liberal leaders, Pedro de Sotomayor. Lorca elaborates the tragic action around the heroic love that Mariana Pineda feels for the man she has aided to escape from prison, and for whose freedom and safety she later gives her life. For Lorca, the historical Mariana Pineda was only his starting point. More important was the legendary heroine, the Mariana Pineda of popular imagination that he remembered from his childhood. The legend served Lorca as a way to displace the focus of the plot from the political and historical events in the heroine's life to the intimate sentimental and emotional life she lived as a woman in love. Thus, the historical figure comes to us considerably transformed. Mariana Pineda had seemed to the young Lorca to be 'a marvellous woman whose entire reason for being, whose entire motivating principle [was] her love of liberty' (II, 946). As such, she took shape in his imagination as a woman of exalted and heroic passions, whose theatrical representation would have been realised in the traditional heroic verse forms of the Golden Age classics of the Spanish stage. But Lorca chose another direction for his play, and in that choice he demonstrated relatively early his promise as a writer with original approaches to the problems of the stage.

'In order to create this fabulous creature', Lorca said, 'it was absolutely necessary to falsify history, and history is an unassailable fact that doesn't allow the imagination any out except to adorn it with poetry in its language, and with emotion in its silences and in all the things that form their background. . . . For I sincerely believe that theatre is, nor can it be anything other than, emotion and poetry in its words, in its action and in its gestures' (II, 946–8). What Lorca had in fact done in this play was to turn away from the rhetorical excesses of romantic theatre in verse and of its twentieth-century imitators, and develop a more intimate and natural level of poetic diction. This is not to say that there are not moments in the play that stand out from its normal level of discourse, almost like operatic arias, due to the virtuoso quality of their poetry and the possibilities they present for colourful execution. But the fact is that these moments stand out due to the general sense of heightened but natural speech that prevails as the norm in the rest of the play.

The drama begins with what is really an overture; this is a brief introductory scene where Lorca calls for the costumes to reflect a period twenty years after Mariana Pineda's death, or about 1850. In this brief opening, a chorus of young girls of Granada sing the popular ballad that tells the entire story of Mariana Pineda and of her death. The scene takes place on the very street where Mariana Pineda actually lived, and the children are singing outside a house that we later discover to be the one where Mariana had lived. 'Oh, what a fateful day for Granada', they sing, 'when even the stones shed bitter tears.' Lorca calls for this scene to be set and played in front of a painted backdrop whereon the street scene would be depicted. The entire representation was to be framed with a yellowed border, which Lorca specifies should be like that of an old lithograph. Moonlight adds to the dream-like atmosphere created by the melancholy ballad. Later in the play, as an echo of this overture, and as a portent of the tragedy that will unfold, Lorca has a scene where Mariana's two children sing a different ballad with their nursemaid before going to sleep, one that tells a medieval tale of a maiden who embroiders a pennant for her soldier lover, only to discover that he has already died in battle. Even in the course of the play itself then, our attention is directed to the legendary and poetic quality of what we are watching. The sets, costumes and properties, on the other hand, are meticulously chosen to evoke realistically a precise period. The purpose is not to suggest a documentary representation of history, but to suggest by means of historically accurate detail the sensitivity and feeling of the romantic era in which the drama is set. Lorca himself suggests that the play is in a certain sense a homage both to the historical Mariana Pineda herself, and to the Granada of her era. It is also a homage to an artistic style and sensitivity that is equally removed from the naturalistic prose drama and the 'epic', patriotic historical verse drama of Spain's 1920s. The action of the play itself is further set apart from contemporary spectators in that the performance both begins and ends with the singing of the popular ballad about Mariana Pineda, some twenty years after the heroine's death. This displacement of the drama's main action in historical time is a stylistic device that emphasises the artificiality of the theatrical representation rather than authenticating it in documentary terms. Lorca thereby sets up the tension that is characteristic of theatre, between the imitative recreation of reality before the eyes of the spectator, and the constant and simultaneous indication that what we are seeing is an artistically elaborated and artificial spectacle. The detailed naturalism of the stage production, on the one hand, is played off constantly against the artificiality of the verse dialogue, the framing effect of the ballad prologue and epilogue, and the intensification of the drama's emotional projection by symbolic means on the other hand. Lorca's interest in exploring this most fundamental and characteristic contradiction in theatre – the creation of experience that is at once real and artificial – is indicative of his keen awareness of the possibilities and limitations of the form even as he started out as a writer for the stage.

The central theme of *Mariana Pineda* is the intersection of two passions in the protagonist-lovers: the devotion to a political ideal of liberty on one hand, and to an ideal of romantic love on the other. Essentially the work is an exploration of the motivation and the meaning behind Mariana Pineda's personal sacrifice. All the other characters in the drama are seen to be secondary in this light, and accessory to the disclosure of Mariana Pineda's extraordinary devotion to a love that she puts beyond all else. Her lover, Pedro de Sotomayor, extols the high principles of his fight for liberty under the threat of a brutal tyranny, but he has no real comprehension of the love that fatally binds Mariana to him so much more than to the cause in which she also nevertheless believes. Although his political struggle calls for courage, Sotomayor is cowardly in his failure to comprehend that Mariana's valour is the expression first and most profoundly of her love for him and not for the abstract principle of liberty he is pursuing. Sotomayor and his co-conspirators use Mariana's house as a place to meet, but they escape soon thereafter to the relative safety of England, leaving Mariana to face arrest, imprisonment and death. As Mariana awaits her certain execution, having refused all compromises that might have gained her a reprieve, her love becomes sublimated, independent of the existence of Sotomayor, or any other object; her sacrifice in the end is for love itself.

It is arguable that Lorca first conceived this drama as a work of primary symbolism. One of Lorca's own descriptions of the play uses religious terminology and points to the fact that what he attempted was to dramatise the progressive spiritualisation of his heroine: 'I wish to write a "processional" drama, a simple and hieratic narrative, permeated by evocations, mysterious breezes, like an old-fashioned Madonna with her arc of cherubims.'[2] The final act is an attempt to transform his character through a kind of apotheosis into a pure symbol of love. At the same time, there can be no doubt that Lorca saw his work as one that would also have primary appeal to the senses, in the tradition of all great ceremony. As he put it in the same letter to Fernández Almagro, '. . . the red of the blood will become confused with the red of the curtains. Mariana is a passionate woman to her very core, a person "possessed" . . . She is a Juliet without her Romeo, and [my treatment of her] is closer to that of a madrigal than an ode. In the final act she will be dressed in white, and the entire stage will be set in the same colour.'[3]

The play went through at least three revisions, beginning in about 1923 with its earliest form. As time went on, the actual production of *Mariana Pineda* became increasingly a matter of constant insistence and delicate manoeuvring on the part of Lorca and his friends. By the time the production by Margarita Xirgu was finally set for June of 1927, Lorca's attitude toward the play had changed considerably. Referring to the debut, Lorca wrote to a friend saying that he was 'terrified' and under a tremendous weight. 'Doing a romantic drama was an extraordinary pleasure for me three years ago,' he said. 'Now I see it as somewhat tangential to the rest of my work' (II, 1158). Nevertheless, he was enthusiastic about the collaboration of his long-time friend, Salvador Dalí, who designed sets and costumes. Even with his hesitations about the quality of the play itself, Lorca was abundantly pleased with its production, going so far as to call it 'innovative'.

The actual set for this production was a good deal smaller than the stage opening itself, so the effect was that of a smaller stage set in the middle of a larger one and framed with a border that was meant to suggest the frame of an old lithograph. In the final analysis, whatever weaknesses existed in the script and the plotting of the piece were for one critic at least eclipsed by the splendour of the work's appeal to the eye and the ear. Sebastiá Gasch wrote of the production, 'the yellow of a dress plays off the black of a backdrop. The curves of a sofa are picked up in the curves of a chair. The clock on the wall extends the line of a window. The stripes of a costume play with the stripes on a doorway. And thus on to infinity. A total symphony, a constant orchestration.'[4] Others were more critical, finding problems in the unevenness of the poetry, and in the sporadic dramatic impetus of the play. Moreover, in this premiere production, Lorca had obviously compromised on some of the 'period' detail he called for in his stage directions, but had been most enthusiastic about Dalí's interpretations. Critics, in fact, commented on the anachronistic effect of the authentic period costumes that contrasted with a set that was executed in an avant-garde and anti-naturalistic style. On the whole, however, no matter how negative the individual critical comments may have been, there was general acclaim for the adventuresome and innovative character of the production, and for those lines, verses and images in the play's text that revealed in Lorca an important temperament for dramatic creation.

'Doña Rosita the Spinster' (1936)

It was only the tragic accident of Lorca's death in the summer of 1936 that determined that *Mariana Pineda* (1927) and *Doña Rosita the Spinster* (1935), Lorca's two Granada plays, should have marked his serious debut and his final appearance on the Spanish stage. Whereas Lorca was nearly overcome by anxiety and self-doubt as he tried to have the *Mariana Pineda* manuscript read and accepted for production, the premiere of *Doña Rosita* eight years later found him at the height of his powers as a writer, and still enjoying the great success of *Yerma* which had opened the previous year. The opening of *Doña Rosita* amounted to a major cultural event in Barcelona, and for Lorca and Margarita Xirgu it was the culmination of their long friendship and their rich professional collaboration that had begun when she produced and took the leading role in *Mariana Pineda* in 1927. Again, in 1935 Xirgu was producing Lorca's play and taking the role of Doña Rosita. Her next project with Lorca's theatre would come in exile, and after the poet's death, in her 1945 production of the *House of Bernarda Alba* in Buenos Aires.

Francisco García, the poet's brother, has said that he believes *Doña Rosita* was written in order to compensate for what Lorca considered privately to have been the failure of *Mariana Pineda*, and as a conscious effort to overcome the weaknesses of this earlier play of Granada. Whatever the reason for the unusually long gestation of this play, *Doña Rosita* certainly marks Lorca's achievement of mature genius as a poet-dramatist. Lorca is in full command of his art in *Doña Rosita*, and able to attain a remarkably subtle blending of poetry and realism, of tragedy and comedy, and to use a wide range of resources, including music, dramatic symbolism, popular poetry, and naturalistic prose dialogue in doing so.

The source of inspiration for this play was innocent enough: Lorca began with nothing more than the verse description of a unique variety of rose that a friend and fellow poet had discovered in an early nineteenth-century botany book. The verses were brought to Lorca's attention in 1924, and the play took shape in his imagination almost instantly. He seems to have taken particular care with this work's elaboration, perhaps initially thinking of it as a post-romantic or modernist verse drama, but then not trusting that particular formal direction after his experience with 'romantic' verse drama in *Mariana Pineda*. The final form that *Doña Rosita* took seems to have depended on the accumulated experience Lorca gained with all aspects of the theatre between 1924 and 1935. It is like nothing else that he produced for the stage.

The most elaborate of any of Lorca's titles introduces us to the precious world of this play: *Doña Rosita the Spinster, or, The Language of the Flowers; A Poem of Granada in 1900, Divided into Several Gardens, With Scenes of Song and Dance.* Grau Sala's poster for the Barcelona premiere complements perfectly the gentle parody of the titles: the lettering is in a flowing cursive hand, and Rosita is surrounded by a swirl of white doves, stars and graceful flowers and vines. It resembles an antique greeting card and is indicative of the care that was taken overall in this production to reproduce evocative elements of the popular culture of each historical period depicted in the three acts.

The flower whose life cycle forms the central symbolic structure of the play, and which is identified inextricably with Rosita, even to her very name, is the *Rosa mutabile*.

The poetic description of the flower is carried directly into the drama when Rosita's uncle, an amateur botanist, berates the family housekeeper for having broken a leaf on this, his most cherished rosebush. The uniqueness of this rare variety, and the terms of its symbolism in the play are first disclosed as the uncle reads aloud the sentimental description of the *Rosa mutabile* which he has found in a book on flowers. This special rose opens in the morning, 'red as blood', blooming full in the sunshine of mid-day; but as 'the long day swoons among the violets / of the sea', the rose turns white, and as the light begins to fade, 'there, on the very edge of darkness, her / petals start to fall'.[5]

As was the case with *Mariana Pineda*, Lorca was concerned with scenic detail, specifying above all the costumes for the main characters. If the staging in general is less elaborately described here than in his earlier play, it may have been due to the confidence he had that he would personally oversee the production of *Doña Rosita*. Lorca himself sought out and acquired all the necessary properties and supervised every detail of the staging, including the music, which he composed using waltzes for the most part to highlight the dreamy and melancholy atmosphere with a melodic style that was also historically authentic. Lorca's brother Francisco described the playwright as he worked on the final version, surrounded by almanacs and magazines from around 1900. The ballad that is sung in act two about the language of the flowers is taken from an authentic manual of the period which included as well, the 'languages' of fans, stamps, gloves, hours and dreams. This play and *Mariana Pineda* are Lorca's most elaborate 'period pieces', but in *Doña Rosita*, Lorca shows that he has become the master of a subtle realism. Rather than remaining at the level of naive reproduction, this play moves constantly beneath the surface by means of a carefully wrought irony that comments on every detail we see and every word we hear. If in *Mariana Pineda* Lorca was learning to use the stage's resources for scenic composition, in *Doña Rosita*, he succeeds in creating scenic effects that seem to comment on their own anachronism, while on another level they are precisely co-ordinated with the play's plot to create a primary emotional impact on the audience. In the final analysis, perhaps it is precisely this capacity to provoke judgement along with emotional response that marks the real maturity of Lorca's achievement in this play. *Mariana Pineda* attempts to be direct and strong in its appeal to the senses and the emotions, in the style of nineteenth-century Romanticism; *Doña Rosita* is subtle and oblique behind its calculatedly ingenuous façade of dated preciosity.

What Lorca had once said of his *Yerma* (1934) could also be said of *Doña Rosita*: '[this play] has no plot as such, although at times it may seem to'. The first act is set in 1885. Rosita, an orphan, is living with her aunt and uncle. Her suitor, a cousin, must leave for Argentina to take care of his family's estate there, and the act ends with a lyric duet between Rosita and her cousin in which she promises faithfully to wait, and he vows to return. She is dressed in bright pink in this act and is about twenty years old. Act two takes place in 1900. To judge from the conversation we hear among the secondary characters, the world beyond the house and beyond Granada has changed. 'Progress' is the watchword of the new century. But all of this is entirely irrelevant to Rosita who anxiously waits for the mail each day, hoping to have news from her fiancé in Argentina. She wears a pink dress whose new style reflects the passage of time, but there is a faint hint of age beginning to fade her charm. Finally, act three shows the most drastic change of any. The year is 1911, and Rosita is a mature spinster whose eyes have a far-off glow. Her dress, again showing the change of style after eleven years, is now a paler shade of pink. The uncle has died and the three women are alone. They are dismantling the house and preparing to move to a smaller place that they can afford in their difficult situation. Rosita is doubly humiliated. She is deeply ashamed of her spinsterhood, and she is mortified at having to leave her home and its gardens. It is in this final act that the most delicate tone of the play is established and maintained. The consequences of Rosita's faithfulness are plain to see. She has become, in Lorca's words, 'that grotesque and moving spectacle, an old maid in Spain' (II, 1009). The play ends on a sustained note of melancholy hopelessness as the women leave the house, and the stage stands empty with the white curtains at the open French doors billowing in the breeze.

Although Lorca may have had the play's outline quite clearly in mind from the very beginning, there is reason to believe that the real difficulty of the work was its tone, and that this could only have been achieved by Lorca in 1935 after more than a decade of writing and directing. While in the process of writing, Lorca calls this play a 'comedia', and says it will be a work of 'gentle ironies, and of compassionate shades of caricature . . . a bourgeois comedy with subdued tones and, infused throughout with the grace and delicacy of past times and different epochs' (II, 970). The following year Lorca described the subject of his work as follows: '[this is] a work into which I have put my very best thinking . . . It has to do with a tragic thread running through our social life: Spanish women who are left spinsters . . . I am focusing on the entire tragedy of Spanish provincial pretentiousness [*cursilería*][6] . . . It is something that will make members of our younger generations laugh, but it really contains a deep social drama because it reflects what our middle class used to be' (II, 975). 'Irony', 'caricature', 'bourgeoise comedy', 'tragedy', 'social drama' – Lorca used all these terms to describe the play at one time or another, and in remarks made on the eve of the play's premiere, he used the word 'comedy', but then quickly revised himself to call it a 'drama of Spanish *cursilería*'. Finally, it was to his brother Francisco that Lorca made what is perhaps his most revealing observation about *Doña Rosita* when he said: 'If in certain scenes the audience doesn't know what to do, whether to laugh or to cry, I will consider that a success'.[7]

It is undoubtedly easier to see the comic elements in this play, the slight exaggerations and the mild caricature that Lorca applies to his depiction of the lives of his characters. For example, the three Spinsters who visit Rosita with their mother, ludicrously overdressed with huge hats decorated with old feathers, epitomise the melancholy plight of women struggling to maintain what they value as a dignified position in society and sacrificing everything to be able to afford to do so. The scene of the Spinsters' visit in act one exemplifies the mingling of comic elements (the physical appearance and banal chatter of the Spinsters), and elements of pathos (the widowed mother's sad sacrifices to maintain her aging daughters in a perpetual and hopeless eligibility for marriage). The already elaborate tonalities of this scene are even further enriched by the arrival of the Ayola girls, the well-to-do and stylishly dressed daughters of a successful photographer. Up to this point, the satire of the Spinsters has been without any excess that would make them seem grotesque. The audience's sympathies and interest are already directed to Rosita's increasingly sad situation, which is precariously close to that of the Spinster sisters; any comic response the spectator might have to the satire of the Spinsters is thus tempered by a sense of melancholy foreshadowing where Rosita is concerned. When the Ayolas enter, however, the satire attains a new level through Lorca's ingenious use of these frivolous girls' mirthful response to the presence of the affected Spinster Sisters. This response becomes contagious, and promptly affects Rosita; ultimately, it must reach the audience and pull it spontaneously into the scene 'on the side of' the girls and Rosita, leaving the Spinsters as isolated objects of general satire. The Ayola girls are gay and noisy, even somewhat vulgar, in contrast to the solemn and pretentiously formal Spinsters. They represent the optimism and childish confidence of young women who are secure in their wealth and its consequent social standing, and who have no concern about being able to make a good marriage when the time comes. It is obvious from the start that the Ayolas consider the Spinsters to be ridiculous to the point of hilarity.

When, for instance, the third Spinster sadly reflects on how, since her father's death, she has lost the pleasure she used to have in playing the piano, the second Ayola facetiously presses the sisters for more detail:

SECOND AYOLA (*with humor*): I remember sometimes his (*the father's*) tears would fall.
FIRST SPINSTER: When she played Popper's 'Tarantella'.
SECOND SPINSTER: And the 'Virgin's Prayer'.
MOTHER: She had so much soul.
(*The Ayolas, who have been containing their laughter, burst out now in great peals. Rosita, turning her back to the Spinsters, also laughs, but controls herself.*)
AUNT: What naughty girls! (*5 Plays*, 163–4)

At last, somewhat ashamed of their impertinence, the Ayola girls try to excuse their uncontrollable mirth with a transparently fabricated story, but the anecdote only provokes the 'start of a light faint laugh of weary and sad complexion' on the faces of the Spinsters.

The Ayolas are more spontaneous and infantile in their satirical fun than they are cruel, but Lorca's keen sense of drama makes this scene one where the isolating power of laughter divides the stage between those who are laughing and those who are being laughed at. The laughter directed at the Spinsters spontaneously embraces Rosita and then the audience as well, and the tragic irony of the scene does not begin to emerge until there is time to reflect on the eventuality of Rosita's occupying a position in society every bit as pathetic and ridiculous as that of the Spinsters. The sharpest edge of this irony, however, is not revealed until we see the full extent to which Rosita herself is and has all along been conscious of her increasingly sad and foolish situation as a woman abandoned by a man, but living in the naive hope for reunion that everyone but she seems to know is illusory. The discovery of the extent to which Rosita has been aware of the falseness of her position, but has also been trapped by the shame of facing the bleak truth of her permanent spinsterhood, does not come until more than half-way through the final act. But the impact of that revelation has been carefully prepared for and enhanced in anticipation by this complicated scene of mirth and sadness in act two.

The end of the second act is a scene of merriment. A letter has in fact arrived from Rosita's cousin who, though unable to return in person, has nonetheless called for them to be married by proxy. It is a pallid compromise, but serves to buoy Rosita's spirits; she tries to be both realistic and positive about it, saying that he will surely come when he can and that the arrangement 'is just one more proof of how much he loves me' (*5 Plays*, 171). Two contrastive chords are struck in this scene, once more with the purpose of subtly undermining the surface mood. The first is the series of sarcastic and humorous remarks made by the housekeeper about something as arcane to her sensible mind as marriage by proxy. 'And at night, what?' she demands, 'Let him come in person and get married. Proxy! I never heard of it. The bed and its paintings trembling with cold and the bridal clothes in the darkest part of the trunk. Madam, don't you let those proxies come into this house. (*They all laugh*)' (*5 Plays*, 171). The second, and more important chord is introduced at the entrance of the Uncle: 'I have heard everything and almost without knowing what I was doing I cut the only *Rosa mutabile* that I had in my greenhouse. It was still red, "Open full at noonday, she's as / hard as coral"' he announces; and Rosita herself completes the verse that describes the mid-day rose: '"and the sun peers through the windowglass / to see her shine". / UNCLE: If I had waited two hours longer to cut it, I would have given it to you white. ROSITA: "White like the dove, / like the laughter of the sea; / white with the cold whiteness / of a cheek of salt." UNCLE: But still, still it has the fire of its youth.'[8] The precariousness of the moment – Rosita is uncertain in her reaction to this disappointing parody of a marriage – and the subsequent allusion to the proximate death-phase of the symbolic rose, all add an ambiguous and even ominous dimension to an otherwise touching gift. The discordant note that is thus sounded by this symbolically charged moment cannot be dissipated by the singing and dancing of the bright polka that ends the act.

When the final act opens on a scene ten years later, with the Housekeeper carrying boxes and suitcases, it is clear that the final stage of the play's symbolic movement has been accomplished. The clock chimes six o'clock, and then chimes six o'clock again. Time has passed and time has stood still. There is little more that 'happens' in the play as Lorca turns instead to a gradual revelation of Rosita's state of mind, and to a meditation on these sad people who have been left behind by a changing world and defeated by their own changing circumstances. The Aunt has been widowed for six years, and her husband's benign disregard for financial matters has left them destitute. Yet his kindness and generosity that ruined them economically were also rare virtues. These gracious people seem undeserving of the relative hardship they are now to endure, and the shame they are suffering at having to give up the life they have known seems more than they should have to bear.

Lorca brings Rosita on stage only for a brief moment at the beginning of the act, just long enough for the audience to see the effects that age have had on her. The striking visual image is introduced, then removed and allowed to linger in the viewer's memory during the visit of an old family friend. When Rosita enters again, the full impact of this final stage of her life is allowed to take hold. She still wears the pink of a younger woman, though it is now a paler shade than before, and her hair is done in long curls. As inevitably as the *Rosa mutabile* changes during its brief life span, so Rosita has changed. The aged look of her face is almost mocked by the girlish pink of her dress and her youthful hairstyle. The visual correspondence between Rosita and the symbolic rose is carried to its final point in the closing moments of the third act when, just as the women leave their house for the last time, Rosita appears, pale (the 'cheek of salt' of the poem) and dressed in white (*5 Plays*, 190).

Lorca projects in his character in this act a clash of youth and age that is grotesque and yet pathetic and moving. Throughout the final act he attains a tone of melancholy tragedy by revealing a kind of muted and unsuspected heroism of the spirit in his Rosita. Were Rosita to have been as blind to the sad futility of her situation as were the three Spinster Sisters of act two, then her characterisation would remain, as theirs does, at the level of a pathetic but also comic-grotesque caricature. However, Lorca makes us see another dimension to a figure whose depiction otherwise might border on the conventional and stereotypical. The suffocating atmosphere of this bourgeois household in a conservative provincial city determines the inward silent nature of Rosita's struggle, and the tragic profundity of her character consists precisely in her awareness of the hopelessness of her hope, and in the inevitability that, as a spinster, she will come to occupy a role in that society that is the object of derision and pity, bereft of any dignity. The family has discovered that, for eight years, Rosita's cousin had been married to a woman in Argentina, and yet had been so weak as to continue his deceit of Rosita and her guardians with letters and promises. Had Rosita merely believed this cruel charade, she would have remained in our memory as a pathetic and naive victim. It is Lorca's deeper vision that brings her to declare to her Aunt in the final scene of act three:

ROSITA (*kneeling before her*): I knew everything. I knew that he had married; some kind soul took care to tell me that. And I have been believing his letters with a sobbing illusion that surprised even me. If people had not talked; if you had not learned it; if no one but I had known of it; his letters and his lie would have fed my illusion like in the first year of his absence. But everyone knew it, and I found myself pointed out with a finger that made my engaged girl's modesty ridiculous, and gave a grotesque air to my maidenly fan. Every year

that passed was like an intimate garment torn from my
body.   (*5 Plays*, 184)

There is still another dimension to Rosita's suffering
beyond that of this public humiliation that she must
privately endure. She experiences the same tragic contradiction that is a primary source of dramatic tension
throughout Lorca's work for the theatre, between the
necessity of hope and the knowledge of its impossibility –
and their coexistence in equal vigour within a single
individual. Rosita sees her own soul as the victim of hope,
as the hapless prey of an illusion that, however false, is all
that allows it to go on living, no matter how circumscribed
that life may become:

ROSITA: I am old . . . Everything is finished, and yet, with
all illusion lost, I go to bed and get up again with the
most terrible of all feelings – the feeling of having hope
dead . . . And yet, hope pursues me, encircles me, bites
me; like a dying wolf tightening his grip for the last
time.   (*5 Plays*, 184)

Without hope, then, Rosita's own projection of herself into
the future consists only of the bleak and realistic prospect
of spinsterhood and its shame.

Lorca's interest in the possibilities of realism, even in this
most poetic of his dramas, grows out of his experience with
La Barraca (1932–35) during the Second Spanish
Republic, and his work on *Blood Wedding* and *Yerma*
during those years as well. *The House of Bernarda Alba* is
probably the culmination of this realistic line in Lorca's
work, but *Doña Rosita* stands as perhaps the most subtle
merging of this realism with a theatrical conception that is
at the same time altogether poetic. On several occasions

Lorca spoke of the play's profoundly social dimension and, in the final analysis, there can be no better way to understand the significance of his accomplishment than to see *Doña Rosita* as the most successfully wrought synthesis of the two principal qualities of Lorca's artistic work. While the play's conception is essentially lyric and symbolic, its realisation is inextricably rooted in the most dramatic aspects of daily life and in carefully specified social and cultural circumstances. The deadness of this tightly controlled and isolated bourgeois atmosphere is seen in this play in its most complex and contradictory light. There is a kind and innocent generosity and humanity in Rosita's Aunt and Uncle, and yet they seem like specimens of a culture that has lingered in its final stages of life through the entire quarter-century represented in the play. Like Chekhov's characters, Lorca's are left behind by time and social change in a kind of dream world; they are aware of their own anachronism, but unable to do anything about it. At the same time, they are incapable of looking to the future with anything but a realistic and resigned determination not to surrender altogether to despair. Rosita asks her widowed Aunt what she intends to do now that they must leave behind everything that is familiar in their lives, and the older woman replies that she intends to 'live – and let you take a lesson from me' (*5 Plays*, 183). This almost pathetically diminished quality of spirit ironically amounts to heroism in these pathetically diminished circumstances.

The passage of time in the play, marked by superficial change, only foregrounds the static nature of the social structures that seem to smother Doña Rosita. She is the girl who never becomes a woman in this society, but who becomes old nonetheless; she is the not-quite-woman whose worth in the eyes of others, and consequently in her own eyes as well, is determined by her marital status, her relationship to a man; she is also the female who must suffer all of this in a silence that belies the despair and the shame she feels because others know her situation in this hermetic and restrictive atmosphere. They judge her in the light of class-determined, and gender-specific expectations that distort and stifle the spirit rather than allowing it to flourish. Rosita is a flower grown in a greenhouse (her Grenadine world) and carefully nurtured. Her life-cycle is perfectly predictable, and, for the aesthetics of those whose sensibilities are tuned to the poetic language of the flowers, the cycle has a melancholy beauty. While the play's structure reproduces that same faintly beautiful cycle in its movement through time and in its depiction of character, it also discovers the pain beneath a life that conforms to such an evolution while nurturing illusions that are known to be false.

Thus while the exquisite bad taste of the epoch's popular culture may cause the spectator to smile, Lorca moves the drama beyond the pleasant evocation of the recent past to examine the real anguish and tragic distortions of spirit that were suffered, especially by women in the society he depicts. The effect of the drama is thus the disturbing and contradictory mixture of laughter and tears that was Lorca's declared intention. The play in fact moves deftly and sometimes precariously along the fine line that separates the merely comic-grotesque from the tragic. Women in other of Lorca's plays are also caught in equally oppressive social circumstances, but nowhere else in his theatre do we see such a masterful control of tone, and such a complete harmony of realism and poetry on the stage.

1. Lorca in the uniform of La Barraca Theatre Company with the Barraca poster behind him.

2. Garcia Lorca and Margarita Xirgu, 1936.

3. Portrait of Lorca taken in the Garden of San Vicente, Granada, 1935.

4. Original cast of *The Shoemaker's Wonderful Wife* with Margarita Xirgu as the wife; costumes and sets by Garcia Lorca, Barcelona, 1930.

5. Scene from a performance of *The Shoemaker's Wonderful Wife* at King's College, London.

6. Margarita Xirgu as Mariana in *Mariana Pineda*. Original 1927 production with sets by Salvador Dali.

Affiche par Grau Sala (1935)

7. Original poster for the opening of *Doña Rosita the Spinster*, designed by Grau Sala, 1935.

8. Margarita Xirgu in the original production of *Doña Rosita the Spinster*, Barcelona, 1935.

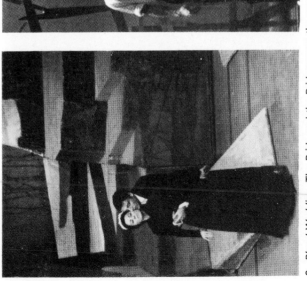

9. *Blood Wedding*. The Bride and the Bridegroom; the wedding scene, Act II. Directed by José Tamayo, Teatro Bellas Artes, Madrid, 1962.

10. *Blood Wedding*. Leonardo and the Bride in the forest scene, Act III. Directed by José Tamayo, 1962.

11. Yerma and María in *Yerma*. From the original production, 1934, with Margarita Xirgu (right) as Yerma. Teatro Español, Madrid.

12. Final scene of *Yerma*; Yerma's murder of Juan, her husband. Production directed by Luis Escobar, Teatro Eslava, Madrid, 1960.

13. *Yerma*. The Washerwomen (Act II), with Yerma looking on. Production directed by Victor García, with set design by Fabian Puigserver, Teatro de la Comedia, Madrid, 1971.

14. *Yerma*. Yerma discovered by Juan in Dolores the Curess' cave. Directed by Victor García, 1971.

15. Yerma and the shepherd, Victor. Directed by Victor García, 1971.

16. Costume design drawing by Lorca for La Barraca production of *The Cave of Salamanca* by Cervantes.

5
The Three Rural Dramas

Blood Wedding and *Yerma* are the first and second plays of
a trilogy 'of the Spanish earth' that Lorca first mentioned in
1933. In 1935, Lorca told an interviewer that the third play
was nearly finished and that those who had liked his last
two dramas – *Blood Wedding* and *Yerma* – would not be
disappointed with this one. There is still some confusion
over exactly what Lorca may have had in mind for this
trilogy. In 1933 he called it a trilogy of the Spanish earth
and included an unknown play called *The Destruction of
Sodom*. In 1934, the same trilogy then included *Yerma*, but
Lorca called the third work *The Drama of Lot's Daughters*.
These are perhaps different titles or ways of referring to the
same project. Only months later (1935), he returned to the
title, *The Destruction of Sodom*, saying that the work was
nearly finished (II, 975). Lorca's good friend, Rafael
Martínez Nadal, also recalls talk of a Biblical trilogy whose
final work would be a drama of Cain and Abel, a fierce
anti-war play in which the 'madness' of the modern world
would be mixed with the biblical legend in strange but vivid

87

superimpositions. 'At first, no one will understand what it's about,' Martínez Nadal reports Lorca as saying.[1] Although not a part of the trilogy that Lorca envisioned, *The House of Bernarda Alba* bears an important relationship to *Blood Wedding* and *Yerma* in as much as they all belong to the last three years, the most productive period of Lorca's work for the theatre, and they are linked by what we may characterise as the progressive refinement of his poetic-realistic drama. Lorca's special concern was to forge a synthesis between realism and poetry in his dramas that would correspond authentically to his artistic concern with form and his equally compelling concern to explore the mimetic aspects of his writing for the stage as well.

In the traditional societies that are depicted in Lorca's rural dramas, convention requires that the union between men and women be one that conforms to the expectations of class continuity and economic stability. In common with Lorca's other plays, the force that drives these three dramas is a relationship between male and female protagonists that in some sense falls outside the bounds of convention.

Blood Wedding (subtitled simply, 'Tragedy') is based on the most drastic violation of sanctioned male-female relationships, that is, the violent abduction of the new bride by her lover on the day of her marriage. *Yerma*, on the other hand, which Lorca called a 'Tragic Poem', represents the profoundly ironic situation of the bride who has happily accepted the conventional expectations of the society in which she lives, but who discovers that her own profoundly felt desire to become a mother will never be fulfilled. Her desire to have a child intensifies almost in direct proportion to the intensity of her realisation of its impossibility. In *The House of Bernarda Alba*, society's values are enforced with a ferocity that has become a part of the consciousness even of those who are oppressed by them. The transgression of the youngest daughter – her attempted flight with her lover – is violently punished, and the prevailing order is dogmatically reasserted.

Eros is a primary force in all three of the dramas, and in *Blood Wedding* and *The House of Bernarda Alba* it has the symbolic role of motivating the clash between sterile convention and deeply felt human passion. In *Yerma* the absence of an erotic force in the relationship between Yerma and Juan underlies her failure to conceive a child, and ultimately defines her tragic condition. Eros is either expressed or subverted in ways that contribute to the fundamental dramatic tension in each play, and it is the symbolic generator of each play's action.

In addition to these thematic similarities, it is tempting when considering these three plays together to see a formal relationship among them. In both *Blood Wedding* and *Yerma*, there are moments where verse replaces prose, and where the rhapsodic speech of a character suspends the movement of the dramatic action in time, while realising a more elaborate expression of feeling. *Blood Wedding* and *Yerma* both have choral sections which perform the same elucidative function that they did in classical tragedy, and both plays also have specific scenes that are based on a dithyrambic outpouring of erotic energy. *The House of Bernarda Alba*, with its sharp focus on detail, and with the almost unrelieved intensity of its dialogue, is formally distinct from the lyrical suggestiveness of either *Blood Wedding* or *Yerma*, and, in a formal sense, seems to stand apart from the first two of this group of plays.

Francisco García Lorca holds that *The House of Bernarda Alba* is in fact the culmination of the whole development of his brother's dramaturgy, and that it had been his conscious purpose to 'prune' away lyric branches in order to achieve this crystallisation, this reduction of his work to 'values of strict dramatic poetry' (*3Trs*, 12). The implied distinction between 'lyricism' and 'dramatic poetry' is an important one. For all their differences, Lorca's last complete plays, *Doña Rosita* and *Bernarda Alba*, are comparable in so far as in both of them he seems to be striving to achieve a more naturalistic representation of social and individual reality. But these final plays are no less poetic in their conception and execution, however, simply because their 'lyric branches' have been trimmed. A common element in both – despite their substantial difference in tone – is Lorca's use of precise details of staging both for their documentary and their allusive and symbolic qualities. *Doña Rosita* and *Bernarda Alba*, written within a year of one another, can both be seen as part of a single experiment by Lorca which involved the refinement of surface naturalism to the point where it would simultaneously serve a poetic or symbolic function in these plays. The dramatic text is still a concentrated and structured illusion whose final purpose is not to reproduce natural speech and activity, but to reveal or to allude to the inner lives of the play's characters and their relations to one another and to the world. Moreover – and this is where Lorca discovered the crucial intersection of poetic and theatrical art – the dramatic text and its realisation on stage must provoke in the spectator a response that is at the same time an intellectual as well as an emotional understanding of the action that is represented.

'Blood Wedding' (1933)

A marriage is negotiated according to custom between two eligible young people who are designated in the playscript simply as the Bride and the Bridegroom. The Bridegroom's mother consents although she has serious reservations about her son's future wife who was once courted by Leonardo, a member of the Félix clan. This clan was responsible for the murder of the Bridegroom's father and older brother. The Bridegroom dismisses this as something better left forgotten; the Mother's apprehensions only increase with time. The Bride's consent in the marriage arrangement is also accompanied by deep anxiety; she is still secretly in love with Leonardo, who is now married to another woman. On the day of the wedding, the Bride and Leonardo flee together and are pursued by the Bridegroom and his family. There is a duel with knives in which both the male rivals die. The play ends with the women – the Bride, the Mother and Leonardo's wife – mourning their lost men.

The crisis of this drama is centred in the contradictory movement and clash of the two principal lines of action: one toward the celebration of the socially sanctioned union between the Bride and the Bridegroom, and another toward the consummation of an illicit and erotically driven relationship between the Bride and Leonardo. These opposed movements of the dramatic plot correspond to the collision of two principles by which men and women are brought into relationships with one another: the first is the marriage union by which the society guarantees continuity within families and classes, and assures the increase and regular transfer of material property; the second obeys only the volatile demands of erotic desire and recognises no restrictions of social class or material circumstances. The first is a principle of order and coherence, and it has the authority of a moral absolute; the second is a force that threatens that authority with the chaos of passion, and the energy of rebellious defiance of social boundaries and moral strictures. The Bride is the character who suffers this dissonance and contradiction most acutely; her struggle becomes a focal point of dramatic interest as the opposed movements of the action – one actual, the other potential – contend within her throughout the second act.

The Mother is the other focal point of dramatic interest. She has lost both her husband and her son to a violent confrontation with members of the Félix clan. She has an obsessive horror of weapons and fears more than anything else the thought of losing her last son as she lost her other two men. At the same time, she is obsessed with the thought that the murderers have not suffered sufficiently for their acts:

> MOTHER: Can anyone bring me your father back? Or your brother? Then there's jail. What do they mean, jail? They eat there, smoke there, play music there! My dead men choking with weeds, silent, turning to dust. Two men like two beautiful flowers. The killers in jail, carefree, looking at the mountains. *(3 Trs, 35)*

The Mother suppresses what seems to be an irrational uneasiness about the Bride's suitability for her son, and she consents to the marriage in the interest of his happiness. But having consented, she discovers that the Bride's mother, now dead, had been beautiful and proud, and it was rumoured that she did not love her husband. The solitary and mysterious personality of the Bride only gives more weight to the Mother's intuitive apprehensions. Though the Mother tries to quell her subjective dread of the marriage, her expressions of rage against the rival clan and the killers of her men, and her suspicious treatment of her son's betrothed, establish early in the play a sense of impending crisis.

The three scenes of the first act occur in distinct locations, and each one sets in motion the conflicting forces that suggest the play's tragic potential. The first scene, between the Mother and the Bridegroom, her son, reveals her complex emotions concerning the proposed marriage, in contrast with her son's lighthearted optimism. The second scene takes place in Leonardo's house, where his wife and her mother are singing a lullaby to a sleeping infant. Leonardo appears, and the news of the Bride's impending marriage provokes a sullen and angry mood in him. He responds with hostility to his Mother-in-law's questions about his long, unexplained absences from home, and finally, he storms out of the room, waking the baby as he goes. The scene begins and ends with a lullaby, but one whose imagery of frustration, apprehension and obstruction is as portentous as Leonardo's intense anger. The final scene of act one takes place at the distant and isolated cave-house of the Bride. The formal negotiations of the wedding agreement are held between the Bridegroom's Mother and the Father of the Bride. The personal qualities that the Father praises in his daughter are actually those of a household servant and a bearer of offspring. The Bride then enters, solemn and quiet, and stands with her hands fallen 'in a modest pose' and with her head bowed. She responds laconically and obediently to the Mother's stern interrogation:

> MOTHER: . . . do you know what it is to be married, child?
> BRIDE (*seriously*): I do.
> MOTHER: A man, some children and a wall two yards thick for everything else.
> BRIDE: I'll know how to keep my word.   (*3 Trs*, 51–2)

The Bride is submissive and dutiful in the presence of the Mother, her Father and the Bridegroom, but the final segment of the scene includes only the Bride and her

Maidservant, and it reveals in the Bride a repressed strength of body and will that profoundly contradicts her behaviour only moments before. She bites her own hand in anger and frustration, and physically struggles with the servant who picks up one of the wedding gifts out of innocent curiosity. Finding herself the target of the girl's hostility, the servant elicits from her the confession that she is visited at night by Leonardo, and Lorca closes the act with the sound of the lover's horse approaching in the distance.

The second act's opening scene brings the two lovers together on the morning of the Bride's wedding day. The servant is preparing the Bride's wedding costume and brushing her hair, but her chatter about the life of a married woman provokes only hostile and tense reactions from the Bride. The dialogue is abruptly cut off as Leonardo appears in the entryway. The illicit nature of the lovers' relationship is dramatised now by the servant's horror at Leonardo's bold intrusion into the Bride's house, and by the Bride's defiant appearance before him dressed only in her petticoat. The scene between the two is filled with bitter accusations against one another for their respective marriages, and at the same time it is charged with an erotic energy that makes their separation seem unbearable and unnatural.

The rest of the act takes place outside the Bride's house during the wedding celebration. The opening scene has released the erotic current that will flow steadily beneath the surface of the entire act, finally inundating the stage at the end and sweeping all the characters towards the play's catastrophic denouement in the third act. Lorca calls for the wedding guests to fill the stage with traditional singing and dancing as the community innocently and gracefully honours the new husband and wife. Nothing is left to chance under Lorca's direction of this scene, even down to the meticulous orchestration of the singers' voices.[2] All of this carefully co-ordinated activity serves to objectify the primary momentum of the play's action towards the consummation of the conventional union between Bride and Bridegroom. At the same time, the dialogue among the principal characters is punctuated by indications of the Bride's tense anxiety and the Mother's growing apprehension that this union is doomed to disaster. The festival serves as an increasingly ironic background to what is now becoming the most compelling movement of the dramatic plot, that is, towards an action that will in some way resolve the lovers' desperate situation. Leonardo appears and disappears, always on the periphery of the activity; the Bride's inner struggle becomes increasingly acute as she shows herself to be abstracted from what is going on around her and unable to respond appropriately to any of the good wishes and frivolous chatter of the guests. She at last begs to be excused from leading off the dancing with her husband and takes leave of the festivities to lie down. Shortly thereafter, when the servant cannot find where the Bride has gone, the inevitable course of events is set in motion, and the dramatic pace accelerates precipitously. Questions are asked and anxious suspicions are raised. Then Leonardo's wife enters crying out that she has just seen her husband and the Bride, 'on his horse, with their arms around each other [riding] off like a shooting star!'

Throughout the act, Lorca has maintained the primary movement of the action towards the accomplishment of the marriage. All the while, he has been building beneath the surface the potential contradictory movement of the action to the point where it finally overwhelms the main momentum and replaces it with a new and fatally doomed movement towards the union of the two lovers.

Once the flight of the lovers has taken place, the Mother is confronted with the discovery that her deepest fears about this marriage have all proved true. Her family has once again been affronted by the rival clan and the requirement for revenge suddenly encounters within the Mother her most serious dread, which is that of losing her son to violence. 'Go! After them!' she cries to her son, and then, 'No! Don't go. Those people kill quickly and well . . .' and then, '. . . but yes, run, and I'll follow! . . . the hour of blood has come again' (*3 Trs*, 77–8). The scene ends as the men move off in pursuit of the fugitive lovers.

The final movement of this act is an instance of Aristotelian *peripeteia*, that is, the transformation of one state of affairs into its exact opposite through a necessary or probable sequence of happenings. Lorca had a clear sense of dramatic necessity and of the spectacular effect that could be achieved by building this pattern in a tragedy.

The flight of the Bride and Leonardo is the action that precipitates the violent denouement, as the third act is largely an intense playing out of the inevitable. As the moment of the death of the two male protagonists approaches, however, Lorca moves the representation on to an altogether new plane of theatricality. When the curtain rises on the third act, Lorca has abandoned the stylised realism of the first two acts in favour of a supernatural exploration of the symbolic terms of the drama. The opening set: '*A forest. It is nighttime. Great moist tree trunks. A dark atmosphere. Two violins are heard. Three Woodcutters enter*' (*3 Trs*, 79). This scene was a rather daring move on Lorca's part. At risk is the loss of all the dramatic tension built up in the previous act, but it seems that Lorca wished to build up a tension now on an entirely different level. The Woodcutters comprise the conventional tragic chorus and their severe dialogue orients the spectator's emotions to the exact terms of the tragic action about to take place. The opposed principles of the drama are now articulated from the perspective of the lovers, constituting an important insight into the tragic essence of the action about to be witnessed:

2ND WOODCUTTER: You have to follow your passion. They did right to run away.

1ST WOODCUTTER: They were deceiving themselves, but at last blood was stronger.

3RD WOODCUTTER: Blood!

1ST WOODCUTTER: You have to follow the path of your blood.

2ND WOODCUTTER: But blood that sees the light of day is drunk up by the earth.

1ST WOODCUTTER: What of it? Better to be dead with the blood drained away than alive with it rotting

(*3 Trs*, 79)

The Moon appears onstage dressed as a young woodcutter with a white face, illuminating the forest with blue light; he sings a ballad of death, and when he disappears, an old Beggar Woman, Death in disguise, comes on to the wooded scene calling for the moonlight to return so that she can seek out her victims. The transposition of the drama on to a plane of poetic symbolism causes the spectator now to see the tragic action purely as a consequence of the collision of antagonistic forces that are inevitably in opposition. Death has now entered the drama as the ultimate antagonist, as the indifferent power that will nullify everything. Nor does Lorca merely isolate this symbolic scene and return again to the formerly established level of representation. The Death figure appears before the Bridegroom and considers him as her prey, and she closes the death scene with the

97

opening of her black cape as the stage is engulfed in darkness. She appears again in the final scene of the play, no longer in the fantastic setting of the forest, but on the doorstep of a dwelling which is also of a design full of symbolic suggestion, where the women gather at the end to lament the deaths of the young men.

Adding to the intensity of the symbolic forest scene is the breathless dialogue between the fleeing lovers. This is a scene of erotic rapture played out almost literally in the shadow of death. The lyric poetry of their final scene is at once a celebration of the lovers' erotic passion and a eulogy to its inevitable termination in death. As they exit in an embrace, the Moon enters very slowly, and the Beggar-woman appears as the stage is lit with blue light again; two shrieks are heard, and the Beggar woman *'stands with her back to the audience . . . opens her cape and stands in the center of the stage like a great bird with immense wings. The Moon halts. The curtain comes down in absolute silence'* (*3 Trs*, 90).

The final scene is almost another act in itself. It opens with a second choral passage where two young girls dressed in dark blue are winding a skein of red yarn against a background of stark white walls. The setting is the Mother's house, but it is meant now to suggest a church, a place where ritual is appropriate: the walls are white as are the stairs, the archways and the floor; *'this simple dwelling'*, the stage directions tell us, *'should have the monumental feeling of a church. There should not be a single gray nor any shadow, not even what is necessary for perspective.'* The girls are speaking in a chanting rhyme, speculating to one another about what may have taken place after the wedding; a third girl appears to announce the approach of the women, and of the men bearing the bodies. The Beggarwoman from the forest scene now appears and she confirms to the girls the deaths of the two young men.

From this point on, the scene is purely elegiac, as the women come together after the killings have taken place. But it is also a scene of symbolic resolution as the three women ironically are united in their grief. The Mother's hatred of the Bride is expressed most devastatingly in her initial physical attack on the girl, and then in her refusal to expiate the Bride's guilt by inflicting further punishment; nor will she acknowledge the helplessness of the Bride to have resisted the course of her passion. The women mourn together, but they are ultimately isolated from one another by their own individual experiences of the tragedy. The Mother's deepest dread has been realised at the same time that she has been swept along by an honour code of violence and revenge. Her son has now followed his brother and father in violent death. Her anticipated peace is tragically ironic: 'I want to be here [in her house]. Here. In peace. They're all dead now: and at midnight I'll sleep, sleep without terror of guns or knives. Other mothers will go to their windows, lashed by rain, to watch for their sons' faces. But not I' (*3 Trs*, 95). The Bride's loss, though less ironic than the Mother's, is as striking in terms of the tragedy as a whole; both these women must live out the consequences of drastic and irreparable reverses of fortune. Leonardo's wife has foreseen the tragedy as her marriage disintegrated in mounting tensions and mistrust. She is now a widow with an infant son and another child yet unborn.

The three women brought together at the end on this glaring white stage symbolically become one. The Mother is at the end of her life, alone; the Bride, in the beginning of her womanhood and widowed on her wedding day, is also alone, but neither a wife nor a mother; Leonardo's wife is at

99

a stage of life intermediate to that of the Bride and the Mother, and she has been 'cast off' by her husband who was restless, careless of her feelings and in love with another woman. As a widow she will repeat the pattern of the widowed Mother, but with added shame. Mother, wife, lover/mistress and bride: all these female roles are symbolically concentrated in this mourning group at the end. The focus of the suffering on the three women, and at last, on the two antagonists, the Bride and the Mother, suggests no resolution. All that is suggested is the uniformity of the destiny of women in the society that is carefully depicted in the first two acts. They are subordinated to men, as daughters and as wives, and without their husbands, fathers and sons, they are nothing. Lorca sees them as the tragic victims, therefore, as those who suffer most acutely from the turbulence and contradictions of a time when principles and emotions are in crisis, and when actions produce the opposite of that which they envisioned or intended.

The repeated allusions to 'blood' in this play call for some explanation of its semantic range in the work. Blood refers to that which relates individuals as groups of kin, as families in a blood line; blood also refers to the inevitable violence of the conventions of honour and revenge in this society where clan justice still prevails. The chorus in act three suggests as well that blood refers to an elemental, instinctual force of life (erotic passion) that draws two individuals together with a compulsion that is as natural as it is fatal; and in the context of the wedding of the second act, blood refers to the breaking of the virgin bride's hymen as the union is consummated. The confluence of these metaphors is dramatically forced where blood is the deadly price that may be exacted for an illicit erotic liaison, where the crime of passion is punished by the violent assertion of the society's retributive code of revenge. The title, 'Blood

Wedding', therefore becomes a metaphoric distillation of the dramatic conflicts that are depicted in the play. Each specific aspect of this symbolism of union – family, kinship, erotic love – discloses through the action of the tragedy its diametric opposite. One set of symbolic meanings for 'blood' undergoes a transformation that is essential to tragedy into a diametrically opposed set of meanings: 'blood', symbolising that which relates and unites and expresses the force of elemental life, becomes a symbol of that which divides, generates antagonism and brings violence and death into human affairs. This aggregation of opposed meanings constitutes the symbolic nucleus of the tragedy.

The premiere of *Blood Wedding* on 7 March 1933, caused a sensation among those who saw the performance. The first act riveted the audience's attention, but the scene in act two with the nuptial celebration, the festive songs and dances, and the growing dramatic tension, provoked an ovation that interrupted the drama and brought a surprised Lorca out for a bow. In fact he was also called out to acknowledge the applause that followed each of the play's three acts.

The critics immediately recognised *Blood Wedding* as a work of innovation for its adventuresome use of an unusually broad range of the theatre's resources. Also impressive was its consistent high seriousness, and its almost classical delineation of the tragic conflict. What people were least prepared for was the mixture of realism and poetic symbolism. Lorca had established the tragic potential of the action during the first two acts in an identifiable social context where specific dissonances and contradictions were driving the action towards a tragic crisis. One critic observed that the elegiac tone of the third act was possibly too intense to carry over such a length of

101

time, particularly when, for the unaccustomed viewer, the other acts, with their poetic passages, might seem overly long as well. Another critic thought that the third act was simply too morbid and lugubrious after the exalted level of tragic tension that had been accomplished in the first two acts. In any case, Lorca's symbolist third act with its elaboration of the tragedy on the level of a clash of the forces of nature and of the human psyche provoked the only reservations that were expressed by contemporary critics.

The more general problem of mixing prose and poetry throughout the play had been an overriding concern of Lorca's in rehearsals, and he tirelessly worked with the cast to maintain a single principle: to make the transitions from prose to poetry as natural as possible by avoiding the declamatory style of acting in verse drama that was the dominant technique on the stage at the time. He had his own vision of the balance that should be sought:

> [*Blood Wedding* is] . . . no more than a dramatic work put together with the rhythmic hammer blows of verse from the first to the last scenes. Free and solid prose can attain high levels of expressiveness, allowing us an outpouring that would be impossible within the rigidity of metrical forms. Poetry is welcome at those moments where the development and the tension of the theme require it. Never at any other time. In accord with that formula, you can see in *Blood Wedding* that up until the epithalamic scene, verse does not appear with any of the breadth and intensity one might expect, and it dominates absolutely the scene in the forest and the drama's final scene.

When asked what he would call the most gratifying part of

the drama Lorca said, 'The one where the Moon and Death intervene as elements and symbols of fate. The realism that predominates the tragedy up to that point is broken and disappears to give way to poetic fantasy where I naturally feel as comfortable as a fish in water' (II, 910–11).

'Yerma' (1934)

Yerma is the second play of Lorca's projected trilogy of the Spanish earth. 'My earliest emotions are bound to the earth and to the labours of the fields', Lorca had said,

> . . . without this love of the earth I could never have written *Blood Wedding*. Nor could I have begun my next work, *Yerma*. I find in the land a profound suggestion of poverty. And I love poverty above all other things. Not sordid and famished poverty, but poverty that is blessed, simple, humble, like black bread.

This vision of Spain's rural people, romanticised though it may be, conveys what Lorca saw and admired, and defines what he made the underlying substance of his rural dramas. The simplicity he speaks of has to do with the elemental level of material life that is represented in these plays, less as a reality than as an ethos that was being lost. Such a view of these dramas overlooks, as Lorca was prone to do, the considerable stylistic sophistication and complexities of realisation that the dramas entail. The sophistication and the complexities are all, of course, demanded by the need to produce the illusion of the greatest simplicity and naturalness of production. What we know of Lorca's work with the casts of these two plays points invariably to his meticulous concern with the details of delivery and sound production, and the co-ordination of individual voices and movements in scenes calling for large numbers of actors and actresses. Everything was to be planned and executed with the utmost discipline and with the ultimate goal of achieving a fluency in performance that would allow the integration of the fantastic with the realistic and the natural presence of music, dance and verse. The plays, in fact, make great demands on the cast. Lorca's statements about *Yerma* indicate that he was seeking a purity of form that was linked to his conception of tragedy:

> *Yerma* is a tragedy. A tragedy in the true sense. From the first scenes, the audience will recognise that something formidable is going to happen. . . . What does happen? *Yerma* has no plot. *Yerma* is a character who develops over the course of the six scenes that comprise the drama. As befits a tragedy, I have included in *Yerma* a chorus that comments on the action, or the theme of the tragedy, which is its real substance. Notice that I have said *theme*. I repeat that *Yerma* has no plot. At several points the audience will think that there is one, but it will be a slight illusion. . . . (II, 979)

Lorca's subtitle points the direction his work is to take: *Yerma* is 'a tragic poem in three acts and six scenes'.

The play's text is for the most part in prose, with lyric verse reserved only for the songs. Yerma's major speeches, however, produce the effect of fine dramatic poetry: they are rhapsodic, giving expression to Yerma's most intensely felt emotions, and they introduce a series of images that are repeated and developed around the main theme throughout the drama. Lorca stated his intention as the play's director to avoid having the actors and actresses speak their lines naturally. Certainly Lorca had declared himself the champion of simplicity in style and the enemy of the histrionic, declamatory method of delivery that was the stock-in-trade of so many of the 'virtuoso' actors and actresses of the day. But he also wished to avoid losing the full resonance of the carefully wrought prose and verse in this play by allowing it to be spoken as though it were ordinary speech. Lorca, in other words, does not disguise the pure theatricality of his tragedy, and his purpose is clearly to establish and sustain serious demands on the audience's sensibilities and attention. The hint of artificiality in the delivery of the speeches, along with the expressive power of their rich imagery, together introduce the element of unfamiliarity that requires an audience to sharpen its receptivity to the nuances of elaborate speech and to apprehend the dramatic experience on all levels at once: on the level of poetic speech, on the level of stylised movement and use of the body, and on the level of the plastic qualities of the staging, costuming and lighting. Lorca was firm in his sense of the play's authenticity and the significance of the values it would introduce to the Spanish stage: 'I would like to think that *Yerma* is something entirely new, in spite of the fact that tragedy is an ancient genre. In *Yerma*'s wake, twenty or thirty years of "art theatre" will be swept away' (II, 997).

This play presents a significantly different configuration of individual and social forces than either *Blood Wedding* or *The House of Bernarda Alba*. Unlike the youthful heroines of the other two tragedies, Yerma's expectations for herself are not altogether in disaccord with those of her society. She has accepted an arranged marriage out of obedience to duty, but also with joy, and with the anticipation that she will find her own fulfilment within the bounds prescribed by her position as a married woman. But this marriage, while formally proper in every other respect, cannot produce children, which is the single most important element in Yerma's conception of herself as a woman. Her sense of inherited honour and duty to her husband is every bit as strong as her desire to bear children; the only solution to her dilemma, therefore, lies with her husband, and he is both deaf and blind to her anguish. The tragic contradiction in this play is thus concentrated in a single character, and her heroic and tragically solitary struggle is against the gradual loss she experiences of her sense of who she is, and of what her purpose on earth might be. In Yerma herself, Lorca has combined the highest possible sense of moral responsibility to conventional society and to herself with a condition of barrenness that can find no solution consistent with her moral convictions. It is the impossibility of Yerma's achieving a resolution to her suffering that is at the heart of the tragic experience. But the critical power of tragedy consists not just in its representation of the conditions that produce suffering, but in its simultaneous vision of the dimensions of social life and consciousness that have been lost, forgotten or are yet to be achieved and that could eliminate such suffering. The issue in Lorca's tragedies is not one of a cosmic fatality that governs the characters' lives; instead, they discover those circumstances of life and consciousness whose effects *seem* to the sufferers to be the workings of a blind and unalterable destiny.

When the curtain rises on the first act, the audience is shown a symbolic tableau that is like no other scene in the entire play, and yet it immediately focuses attention on the interior world that is the real subject of the tragedy to follow. Yerma is asleep and her dream is represented in a fleeting and wordless vision. '*The stage is in the strange light of a dream. A shepherd enters on tiptoe, looking fixedly at Yerma. He leads by the hand a child dressed in white. The clock sounds. When the shepherd leaves, the light changes*

*into the happy brightness of a Spring morning. Yerma
awakens.*' As the light comes up, a nursery song is heard
being sung in the distance. Yerma's dream, innocent,
lyrical, perhaps enigmatic at the beginning of the play,
becomes increasingly obsessive and overpowering through
the three acts.

The symbolic dream gives way to the sunlight of a spring
morning. Yerma awakens her husband Juan, who prepares
to go out to work in his fields. The entire first act, almost in
a musical sense, will be a restatement and elaboration of
the theme that has been suggested in the dream prelude.
Yerma expresses her concern over the effect that long
hours of physical labour are having on Juan. She sees his
strength being drained from him, in contradiction to what
should be the case with a young man recently married and
at the peak of his powers. But Yerma's expressions of
concern soon produce tension in Juan, and he answers
sharply and defensively: '. . . There's nothing wrong with
me. All these things are just your imagination. I work hard.
Each year I get older' (*3Trs*, 104). The tension between
them increases as the subject of their childlessness is
suggested, and Juan leaves for work, reiterating that
Yerma's place is in the house while he is absent. In the
manner of a soliloquy, Yerma then sings a song to herself as
she sews; it is a lyric evocation of the child she longs to bear,
sung as though she were speaking to the child before its
birth. She seems to conjure the child in her rapture as
though she were dreaming again, but nothing is seen or
heard this time.

The first act is built around three encounters between
Yerma and other characters. Each one suggests by symbolic contrast or by allusion a new way of seeing the theme
of Yerma's childlessness that has been stated at the
beginning of the act. As Yerma's song ends, María enters.

She has been married five months and is bearing a child. Yerma expresses her delight and she talks eagerly about children. But at the same time, she cannot avoid expressing her own sadness. Yerma is apprehensive not only about how long she has been married without conception, but also about what will happen to her with time, if she does not conceive. 'Every woman has blood for four or five children,' she says, 'and when she doesn't have them, it turns to poison' (*3 Trs*, 108–9). The innocent, natural fulfilment that María experiences in her marriage and her pregnancy forms a counterpoint to Yerma's unsatisfied longing; María's naïveté stands in ironic contrast to Yerma's knowledge.

When María leaves, Víctor enters. Seeing Yerma working on the sewing that María has brought for her to do, he assumes that it is for Yerma's own child that must be on the way. He is pleased for her, but she then confesses to him that the clothes are for María. This brief scene is full of poignant irony, as Yerma's anguish again comes to the surface. Víctor disarms the tension by saying half in jest that Juan should think less about his work and more about having children to whom he can leave his property. At the end of the scene, when Víctor leaves her, Yerma sings to 'her child' again, then moves to the place where Víctor has stood just moments before and breathes deeply *'like one who breathes mountain air'*, as Lorca's directions tell us. This suggestive scene with Víctor (who is *'deep looking and has a firm gravity about him'*) is the first hint towards that sense of plot that Lorca said would emerge at certain moments, only to prove an illusion. The gentle shepherd, Víctor, seems to disturb and attract Yerma all at once. This allusion to a potential ideal harmony between them is restated at the end of this act even more concretely and in direct contrast with the discordant note struck by the entrance of her husband Juan.

The second scene of act one takes place in the fields as Yerma carries food out to her husband. On the way she meets an old woman, from whom Yerma seeks the answer to the enigma of her barenness. The old woman has borne fourteen children with two husbands. By way of symbolic contrast to Yerma's sombre obsession with her own deficiency, the old woman projects an image of natural fecundity which allows her a spontaneous and unreflective attitude towards erotic experience, and towards life in general. When the old woman's questions discover the fundamental absence of erotic passion and pleasure between Yerma and Juan, Yerma reveals her own inability to recognise that this could have anything to do with her failure to conceive. Her declaration ends with an image of her own sense of sterile frustration and entrapment in a relationship that without children is locked in a meaningless (for Yerma) kind of narcissism:

> My husband is something else altogether. My father gave him to me and I took him. With happiness. That's the plain truth. Why from the first day I was engaged to him I thought about . . . our children. And I could see myself in his eyes. Yes, but it was to see myself reflected very small, very manageable, as if I were my own daughter.
>
> (*3Trs*, 113)

To the old woman, however, it is clear: there is no free and instinctive response to erotic pleasure in Yerma's relationship with Juan, and thus there can only be sterility where conception is concerned. 'Men have got to give us pleasure, girl. They've got to take down our hair and let us drink water out of their mouths. So runs the world.' To which Yerma replies, 'Your world, but not mine. I think of a lot of things, a lot, and I'm sure that the things I think about will come true in my child. I gave myself over to my husband for his sake, and I go on giving to see if he'll be born – but never just for pleasure' (*3 Trs*, 113). Yerma cannot obtain the wholeness she seeks in motherhood because the relationship she has with Juan is only fragmentary, refusing the element of mutual pleasure, admitting only the ideal project of the child. Yerma approaches the old woman as a source of traditional wisdom, but the old woman's words are like riddles whose truth Yerma cannot decipher. Failing to understand, Yerma's alienation only increases. 'Girls like me who grow up in the country have all doors closed to them', she tells the old woman, 'everything becomes half-words, gestures, because all these things, they say, must not be talked about' (*3 Trs*, 114).

Yerma now encounters two young girls in the fields. One has a child at home, and when Yerma chides her for leaving him unattended so long she becomes alarmed at her own irresponsibility and runs home. The Second Girl is married and childless, but represents a dramatic contrast to the melancholy contradictions of Yerma's situation. She lightheartedly disdains marriage as an oppressive institution, with its social restrictions, its duties and complications of child-rearing. Lorca presents her as an outspoken and exuberant young woman, with an attractive truthfulness to her clear and critical perception of the world of conformity and convention: 'I'll tell you the only thing I've learned from life: everybody's stuck inside their house doing what they don't like to do. How much better it is out in the streets' (*3 Trs*, 115–16). Yerma, on the other hand, has accepted without compromise the duties and restrictions of being a wife, but with the singular and unrelenting goal of creating new life out of that socially determined relationship with a man. For Yerma, the only meaning that individual life can have consists in its very conformity to what she sees as laws of nature, and specifically, in life's capacity to create more life, to reproduce, renew and perpetuate itself. By contrast to Yerma, and in spite of her compelling insight and rebellion against repressive tradition, the Young Girl's insistence on her own freedom, pleasure and caprice seems ultimately to form a negative polarity to the more integrative sense of order and purpose that Yerma seeks in her own life in society and in nature. 'You're only a child', Yerma tells her as she leaves.

The act closes with a second scene between Yerma and Víctor. First, only Víctor's voice is heard singing, and Yerma listens, waiting. Víctor is a shepherd, he is a singer, and he exudes an optimism, vitality and candour that form a symbolic contrast to Yerma's Juan, a tiller of the soil, bound to his work that wears him down, and whose concern with honour and external form makes Yerma's situation seem all the more occluded and hopeless. Yerma has admitted to the Old Woman before that the only time she has ever felt the stirrings in her body of feeling for a man was with Víctor when they were younger, and this encounter therefore has the added dimensions of an unspoken courtship and a silent struggle between the two. Yerma, trembling with emotion in the presence of Víctor, believes that she hears a child crying, but Víctor says that he hears nothing. The elements of the dream that opened the play are all present for Yerma here – the shepherd and the child – and this time, her imagination needs only to suggest the child. At this fragile moment, Juan appears and bitterly warns Yerma about being seen outside the house talking to others. Yerma responds to him bitterly as well and he sends her back home, telling her that he must stay in the fields all night to irrigate his land.

Yerma has appeared in this act as a young woman, still hopeful that she can communicate her overwhelming need to her husband, and seeking answers to the condition that she feels sets her apart from all of nature. Her anguish intensifies as her desperation grows over the succeeding two acts; 'plot', in the traditional sense of a sequence of related and interdependent dramatic actions, is found only in the faintest of outlines. 'Plot' is almost entirely subordinated to the creation of a heightened poetic discourse – in terms of both language, and symbolic action – whose singular intention is to elaborate, ever more intensely as the play progresses, the emotional experience of the protagonist. Yerma will speak rhapsodically of her dream and her desire, and she will often seem to speak in apostrophe, elaborating her ideal and expressing the conditions of her suffering. This quality of speech is precisely what Lorca was alluding to when he insisted that the cast should not deliver their lines 'naturally', emphasising the heightened emotive effect he wished to achieve in all phases of the play. The poetic quality of the work begins with its speech, of course, but it also resides in the overall movement towards simplicity of design and richness of verbal and dramatic imagery.

The choral scene opens the second act. When originally performed this scene provoked the most consistent expressions of enthusiasm from audiences and critics alike. In contrast to the symbolic fantasy of the forest scene in *Blood Wedding*, the premise of this scene in *Yerma* is entirely plausible. Six washerwomen are working besides a mountain stream. The scene is full of life, colour and music as the women sing and gossip while they wash. They know everything about Yerma's unhappiness and symbolically dramatise public curiosity and speculation concerning Yerma's natural attraction to Víctor. They also introduce, without resolution, the contradictory allegations of guilt and blame for the continued sterility of Juan and Yerma's marriage. 'She hasn't any children, but that's not her fault', one of the women says, and another replies, 'The one who wants children, has them'. There are veiled accusations that Yerma is looking for 'some man who's not [her] husband', in an obvious reference to Víctor, and '. . . when she's not looking at him – when she's alone, when he's not right in front of her – she carries his picture in her eyes'. 'But what about her husband?' 'Her husband acts like a deaf man. Just stands around blankly – like a lizard taking the sun.' 'It's all his fault; his', another laundress retorts. 'When a man doesn't give children, he's got to take care of his wife' (*3 Trs*, 122).

Motifs from act one are now restated with variations through act two, scene two. Five years have passed between acts one and two, and seven since Yerma's marriage. The passage of time and Yerma's persistent childlessness are major poles of tension. Juan's obsessive concern with his honour has caused him to bring his two maiden sisters to live in the house so that Yerma will not be alone. The sisters, dressed in black mourning, hover in the background throughout the second act, intensifying the sense of Yerma's increasingly circumscribed situation. María enters carrying a child in her arms. To her, Yerma opens her heart and expresses the deep alienation she is feeling from herself, from humanity in general, and ultimately, from all of nature:

I'm hurt, hurt and humiliated beyond endurance, seeing the wheat ripening, the fountains never ceasing to give water, the sheep bearing hundreds of lambs, the she-dogs; until it seems the whole countryside rises up to show me its tender sleeping young ones, while I feel two hammer blows here, instead of the mouth of my child.

(*3 Trs*, 132)

Víctor then enters to say farewell to Yerma and Juan, as he must leave with his brothers to take care of distant properties. While Víctor's disappearance seems to remove from Yerma's life the man who is suggested by her dream and by her experience as her ideal counterpart, and the only hope for the fulfilment of her need for a child, we also realise that he has never been anything other than a symbol and a dream. In the real context of Yerma's life, and given her fierce determination to maintain her husband's as well as her own honour, there was never any possibility that Yerma and Víctor could have been joined. The scene of farewell is elegiac, and one of great delicacy. The loss of the dream, however impossible it might have been, is yet another step in Yerma's journey towards a final confrontation with the absence of hope.

The second act closes in near-darkness as the day ends and Víctor departs. In the gloom Yerma then slips out of the house to meet with the sorceress, Dolores, in what is her most desperate attempt yet to understand and solve the riddle of her barrenness. Juan's sisters enter, lighting the stage only with their lamps, calling for Yerma, who has already gone. Víctor's departure – that is, the departure of symbolic eros, love and fertility, and the symbolic antithesis of Yerma's arid relationship with Juan – is signalled throughout this scene by the 'long and melancholy sound of the shepherds' conch-shell horns' and the ringing of sheep bells along the road as darkness falls. The rich and poetic suggestiveness of this concert of stage action and physical effects can only be compared with the poignant final scene of *Doña Rosita the Spinster* as the breeze flows softly in from the garden through the curtains and through the empty house that the women have just left.

With act three, the play enters the darkest phase of Yerma's evolution as a character. The meeting in the cave

114

of the sorceress (scene one) takes place as dawn is breaking, after the night has been spent in the performance of ritual acts to make Yerma fertile. The Old Woman advises that she should seek refuge in her husband's love while she awaits the action of God's grace. Yerma's response reveals that there is literally nothing that would constitute a fertile relationship between herself and her husband: 'He goes out with his sheep over his trails', she says, 'and counts his money at night. When he covers me, he's doing his duty, but I feel a waist as cold as a corpse's, and I, who've always hated passionate women, would like to be at that instant a mountain of fire.' Yerma's response to her husband's coldness is contradictory: she is repelled by sexual passion, yet wishes that she might feel it if it would serve to solve the dilemma of her childlessness. The lack of passion is mutual. Yerma asserts, moreover, that Juan does not suffer in the least for their failure to conceive a child and she resents his peace: 'He doesn't suffer. The trouble is he doesn't want children! . . . I can tell that in his glance, and, since he doesn't want them, he doesn't give them to me. I don't love him; I don't love him, and yet he's my only salvation. By honor and by blood. My only salvation' (*3Trs*, 140). The scene ends as Juan and his sisters enter Dolores' cave, having searched through the night for Yerma. Yerma's wrath and desperation achieve their strongest expression so far in this confrontation with Juan. She raises her voice in protest and grief, and as others try to silence her, she realises that her voice is the only thing left to her that is not constrained by the oppressive context of her husband's honour and her own lack of fulfilment; the metaphor is that of her voice, the only part of her that is still free, as the analogue to the child that her body cannot create: '. . . at least let my voice go free, now that I'm entering the darkest part of the pit. (*She rises*) At least let this beautiful thing come out of my body and fill the air.' Yerma's resignation is expressed at the end of the scene in terms of her silence: 'It is written, and I'm not going to raise my arms against the sea. That is it! Let my mouth be struck dumb!' (*3Trs*, 143).

The second and last scene of act three is played in a growing darkness that becomes complete as the final, dithyrambic scene unfolds and carries the action to its climax. Whereas the erotic dialogue of the lovers in *Blood Wedding* had taken place in the semi-fantastic world of the forest, in *Yerma*, the celebration of eros is dramatised in the realistic context of a popular festival, the fusion of a Christian pilgrimage to a shrine, and a more ancient, pagan celebration of sexuality and fertility. The scene calls for a crowd of revellers and a chorus of singers and dancers; voices and bells accompany the erotic dance of the symbolic female and male figures. By contrast to this scene of ritual singing and orgiastic dancing, Yerma comes to pray solemnly to the patron saint so that she might by some miracle become able to conceive. Her desperation is manifest in so far as the pilgrimage is made by women who seek the solution to their barrenness less in the act of supplication to the Catholic saint than in their participation in the free sexuality of the pagan celebration that underlies the more recent Christian tradition. Two dancers, one male and the other female, appear wearing masks. They are known as the devil and his wife, and their singing and movements are the ritual representations of the act of sexual intercourse and conception. This scene must be played as an outburst of spontaneous eroticism and contagious sensuality, and Lorca's instructions warn against any element of grotesqueness; the dance must be, *'of great beauty and* [have] *a feeling of pure earth'* (*3Trs*, 147). Lorca's representation of the ritual is meant to evoke enthusiastic contact with the elemental and erotic sources of life in nature, and it contrasts overwhelmingly here with Yerma's ultimately tragic entrapment in the sterile bonds of convention. When the Old Woman offers Yerma her young son as a sexual partner, insinuating that she leave Juan altogether, Yerma's violent rage at the depravity of such a suggestion is the definitive symbol of her enthral-ment: 'Do you imagine I could know another man? Where would that leave my honor? Water can't run uphill, nor does the full moon rise at noonday. On the road I've started, I'll stay . . . I'm like a dry field where a thousand pairs of oxen plow, and you offer me a little glass of well water. Mine is a sorrow already beyond the flesh' (*3Trs*, 151).

Indeed, there is no solution to her childlessness 'in the flesh' for Yerma, and there is no solution to her obsession 'outside the flesh' either. The extreme terms of this contradiction suggest no middle ground; the tragic futility of Yerma's situation is the most awesome of any of Lorca's heroines. When she finally hears from her own husband's lips the assertion that he never wanted children, and when he then drunkenly seeks to take his sexual pleasure with her, Yerma's culminating act in strangling him to death represents the ultimate closure. As with the Mother in *Blood Wedding*, the death of hope is also the supremely ironic release from suffering. 'Barren, barren, but certain: Now I really know it for sure. And one', Yerma says over her husband's body. 'Now I'll sleep without startling myself awake, anxious to see if I feel in my blood another new blood. My body, dry forever!' (*3Trs*, 153). The tension of this murder, which is really a symbolic suicide, is not allowed to dissipate at the end. The curtain falls on Yerma's cry of desperation as the crowd approaches her and her dead husband. Those who saw the initial performances of this play have recorded the stunned silences of the spectators at the end, relieved only after several moments by the ovation.

Yerma and Juan are symbolic of two mutually excluding life principles. He is the materialist, bound to the land in a relationship of work and duty, with no thought of anything beyond what he can see and touch and consume. Yerma, on the other hand, can find no meaning in anything that does not contribute to the achievement of the ideal, the creation of that which does not already exist; for her, there can be no authentic existence that does not seek constantly to transcend its own immediate material strictures through the creation and perpetuation of new life. Thus, her horror of eroticism because she sees only its exclusive focus on the sexual act, with no vision of its procreative essence. Lorca sets the tragic situation in motion by bringing these two alien principles together in a childless marriage. But the real drama consists in the gradual discovery by Yerma of the terrible alienation and distortion that she experiences as the definitive nature of her condition becomes impossible to deny.

Lorca was intrigued both in *Doña Rosita* and in *Yerma* with the possibilities of representing the way in which the human spirit confronts hopelessness with the invention of hope, until, with the passage of time, the inevitable admission of defeat has to be made. Each play is built around the passage of time as the way of bringing forth the inevitable catastrophe; there is really no plot, and no intrigue other than the detailed elaboration through symbolic language and action of the inner experience of the protagonists. At the same time, Lorca was careful to locate the sources of these tragic crises of human relationships in the material and social circumstances of his characters' lives. It was in his final complete drama, *The House of*

Bernarda Alba, that Lorca attained his most powerful representation of the disintegration of human relationships, taking place in the specific context of a social order whose oppression intensifies as its decadence and inhumanity is exposed over the course of the dramatic action.

'The House of Bernarda Alba' (1936)

The House of Bernarda Alba is without question Lorca's most profound contribution to the revolution in the Spanish theatre that he himself repeatedly called for during the 1930s. The play certainly signals Lorca's discovery of a new style of writing for the stage. He is reported to have emphasised in remarks made to friends the 'severity' and 'simplicity' of the play's tone and style, adding that he had consciously suppressed the inclusion of many 'facile songs, ballads and refrains.'[3] He is also said to have exclaimed triumphantly after reading the manuscript to a gathering of friends, 'not a single drop of poetry! Reality! Realism!'[4] As if to underscore this quality of the drama, he subtitled it precisely, 'A drama about women in the villages of Spain', and added after the list of characters, 'The writer states that these Acts are intended as a photographic document'. It is not by any means clear from Lorca's statements, however, just what he meant by 'realism' or by 'photographic document'. It would be a mistake to assume that where either the play's style or its subject matter are concerned Lorca was thinking in terms of a naïve mimesis, or a naturalistic principle of reflective realism. And, in so far as the term 'realism' in theatre may refer to the representation of the emotional lives of people in a complex relationship to a specific cultural, ideological and historical context, and to specific material circumstances, then *Blood Wedding*, *Yerma* and *Doña Rosita the Spinster* may all be said to be as

119

'realistic' as *The House of Bernarda Alba*. But gone from *Bernarda Alba* are the choruses and the dithyrambic-lyric scenes that distinguish *Blood Wedding* and *Yerma*, and gone are the redolent and poignant songs of *Doña Rosita*.

The poetic quality of *Blood Wedding* and *Yerma*, of course, extends beyond those passages that are sung or that appear in verse. When, in *Blood Wedding*, the Mother, Leonardo's wife, the Bride or Leonardo speaks, the attention of the listener becomes focused more on the uniquely structured symbolic language of their speeches, and on the passion it represents, than on the individual character who expresses it. It is the collision of these symbolised passions, more than any factor of individual psychology, that determines the action and that precipitates the catastrophe and the tragic ending in *Blood Wedding*.

In *Yerma*, the lyric mode prevails in the characters' speech to a far greater degree even than in *Blood Wedding*. From Yerma's first innocent and hopeful attempts to communicate to Juan her overwhelming need, to her final outbursts of rage and pain, the lyric transparency of her language is constant. 'Plot' is almost entirely subordinated to the creation of a heightened poetic language whose singular intention is to elaborate, ever more intensely as the play progresses, the emotional experience of the protagonist.

From *Blood Wedding* and *Yerma*, the step that Lorca takes in order to arrive at the kind of dramatic language that prevails in *Bernarda Alba* involves the almost total suppression of the rhapsodic and apostrophic mode of speech that characterises lyric drama, and its replacement with a dialogue of an extraordinary severity and concentration. In *Bernarda Alba*, words serve far more to contain and disguise feelings than to express and elaborate them. This anti-lyrical mode of dramatic dialogue, and the extreme tension between the façade of words and the real feelings behind them, are directly analogous to the play's central metaphor of oppression and the enslavement of the spirit and the will to the uncompromising authority of inherited values. The fact that this oppression and the hostility it produces find expression in occasional and brief outbursts of physical violence only sharpens our perception of the violence of intention that motivates a predominant portion of the characters' speeches, and it increases our dread of the inevitable and definitive violence that ends the play.

The play's title refers to Bernarda Alba's house, thus pointing to the general metaphor of confinement that structures the consciousness of the characters and determines the physical requirements of production. For the January 1964 run of *Bernarda Alba* in Madrid's Teatro Goya (this was, in fact, the play's first performance in Spain), director Juan Antonio Bardem sought above all to convey an asphyxiating sense of insulation from the outside world; this goal led him to exclude some of the decorative detail Lorca had called for, in favour of a more monolithic severity of setting. The entire play transpires inside the rooms of the house, and Lorca calls for the set to include *'thick walls'* with surfaces of brilliant white. The sparkling cleanliness of the varnished floor and the spotless panes of the china cupboard in the first act are the physical analogues to Bernarda Alba's fanatical preoccupation with surfaces and façade.

Bernarda Alba and her family enjoy an economic status superior to that of any other family in this area of rural Spain. Bernarda's dominance over the lives of her five daughters reaches an extreme after the death of her husband, with whose funeral the play opens; the tensions within the walls of the house build steadily over the three acts. As matriarch, she must zealously guard the reputation of her family. In her position of class superiority, Bernarda knows that she is being watched constantly by those below her; not only must she guard her own secrets, but she must know the secrets of others in order to maintain her authority. Her horror of contamination operates at every level, from the marks left on her floor by visitors' feet, to the sexual purity of her daughters and the need to make economically advantageous and socially acceptable marriages for them. Angustias, Bernarda's only daughter by a first husband who died, is about to be wed to a younger man in an arranged marriage. She is nearly forty years-old, the oldest of the daughters, and she is the wealthiest due to her double inheritance. The prospect of Angustias' 'escape' from the household owing only to her economic advantage provokes hostile jealousy among the sisters. Once again, an arranged marriage and its distortion of values and relationships is the plot mechanism that Lorca uses to drive the tragic action toward catastrophe. The prospective husband of the eldest daughter Angustias, is, in fact, also the romantic lover of the youngest daughter, Adela. The representation of Adela's solitary rebellion against the tyranny of the household is far bleaker in its tone than that of the Bride's escape in *Blood Wedding*. Whereas in the third act of *Blood Wedding* Lorca creates the lyrical scene of the Bride's and Leonardo's rapturous and desperate flight, Adela's rebellion holds no hope even for such an ephemeral idyll. Adela's rebellion is hard and relentless, conditioned by the harshness of her mother's authority and by the harshness of the society at large. She is driven by an erotic energy whose only object happens to be this man, El Romano, who will marry Angustias for her wealth. In Lorca's conception of this drama, the detailed portrayal of the intolerable confinement and sterility of the 'society' within Bernarda's house has more importance than any figuration of an ideal society outside its walls. The suffering that Adela says she would endure in exchange for her freedom is the measure of the intolerable repressiveness of her mother's authority:

> I can't stand this horrible house after the taste of his [El Romano's] mouth. I'll be what he wants me to be. Everybody in the village against me, burning me with their fiery fingers; pursued by those who claim they're decent, and I'll wear, before them all, the crown of thorns that belongs to the mistress of a married man.
>
> (*3 Trs*, 208)

As the youngest and most attractive of the daughters, Adela is the least resigned to her future under her mother's domination. But while the pathos of her situation and the desperation of her final act of rebellion do cause her, among all the characters, to be the focal point of the audience's sympathy, Lorca does not create in Adela a heroine of romantic tragedy. She is young, but she is neither innocent nor idealistic. She is desperate, and the corruption of feeling that is evident to a greater or lesser degree in all the daughters is seen in her as well. Her youth is consistent with her symbolic role of rebellion and self-sacrifice in her struggle, but her despair and rage at the impending marriage of her lover, El Romano, to Angustias provoke her into cruel attacks against her older sister. Adela also clashes fiercely with La Poncia, the household servant, and with her sister Martirio, both of whom, for their own reasons, try to obstruct her continuing affair with El Romano. Adela declares to them both that nothing they can do will prevent her from attaining her freedom from the suffocating tyranny, not only of Bernarda, but of her

jealous and frustrated sisters who are fatalistically resigned
to their destiny as Bernarda's daughters and as women. At
the end of the play, Adela confronts Martirio, who is also
secretly and pathetically enamoured of El Romano, and
declares her triumph over the rest of the sisters:

> ADELA: This is just the beginning. I've had the strength to
> push myself forward – the spirit and looks that you
> lack. I've seen death under this roof and gone out to
> look for what was mine, what belonged to me.
>
> (*3 Trs*, 207)

With the play's overriding contextual metaphor being
that of severe physical and psychological restriction, and
with the characters set against one another in a hostile and
jealous competition, the dialogue demands constant
interpretation as to the true intentions of the speaker.
There are moments in the play, nevertheless, where one or
another of the daughters expresses her feelings in a
rhapsodic or lyrical tone, but the effect of such exceptional
moments is immediately and inevitably obliterated by an
especially severe reassertion of the predominantly harsh
tone of the dialogue. Even with the role of Adela, Lorca is
extremely sparing in the moments when he has her express
lyrically the symbolic terms of her struggle. In one such
instance, Adela echoes the verses sung by the itinerant
reapers who pass through the village, and their spontaneous and earthy celebration of eroticism sharpens by
symbolic contrast the play's image of repression. In another
instance, having just seen a falling star while standing in the
patio, Adela asks her mother why people always repeat an
incantation when lightning flashes or they see a falling star.
Bernarda replies simply, 'the old people know many things
we've forgotten', while Amelia, reflecting the timidity of

the sisters, says, 'I close my eyes so I won't see them'. Adela's reply is a clear symbolic reference to her own distinctiveness and unfulfilled longing to escape: 'Not I. I like to see what's quiet and been quiet for years on end, running with fire' (*3Trs*, 201). The star's burst of freedom and its rapid demise also prefigure Adela's own destiny in the play.

In the heavily-walled interior of the house, moments of lyricism are like windows that look out on to another dimension of reality. The most powerful suggestion of this dimension in this play is the figure of the Grandmother. Such is the distortion of feeling represented in the house that the lyrical mode is coincident in this character with madness. Locked away in an interior room, the Grandmother, María Josefa, is the most severely repressed of all the members of the household. Her voice is heard during the first scene calling from within for Bernarda. When she first appears on stage at the end of act one, her presence and her words combine to form a grotesque image of the future of the daughters. The old grandmother has decked herself out with flowers as though she were a maiden or a bride. She is the prisoner of the household, but her words evoke a world that seems ironically remote and idealised, given the context of her own and the daughters' confinement:

MARÍA JOSEFA: I ran away because I want to marry – I want to get married to a beautiful manly man from the shore of the sea. Because here the men run from women. . . . I don't want to see these single women longing for marriage, turning their hearts to dust; and I want to go to my home town. Bernarda, I want a man to get married to and be happy with! (*3Trs*, 175–6)

As though the truth of her vision and the message of her longing were too much for them to bear, all the daughters act as one to subdue her immediately and return her to her locked room.

María Josefa appears for a final time in the closing moments of act three. It is night-time and she has escaped. She finds the jealous Martirio also awake, spying on her sister Adela who will be meeting her lover just outside the house. The Grandmother is singing a strange, plaintive song about an imagined world, and this time, she evokes another dimension of womanhood that the daughters will never know: María Josefa is no longer the bride, but she now carries a baby lamb which she addresses as though it were her child. It is a pathetic and grotesque symbolic parody of motherhood, which is combined once again with the old woman's penetrating vision of the truth: 'Just because I have white hair you think I can't have babies, but I can – babies, and babies, and babies', and she continues to evoke a utopia out of the past where values were simple and universally shared:

> When my neighbor had a baby, I'd carry her some chocolate and later she'd bring me some, and so on – always and always and always. You'll have white hair (*to Martirio*) but your neighbors won't come. ... I like houses, but open houses, and the neighbor women asleep in their beds with their little tiny tots, and the men outside sitting in their chairs.   (*3 Trs*, 206)

María Josefa is Lorca's chorus in this play. Her madness is lucid, and her vision of the sterility and death that dominates the household is so accurate that it must be repressed even by violence. In the context of the distorted world of the household, her expression of an ideal world

126

seems cryptic, visionary and remote, although Lorca really only intends for it to evoke the simple values of community, family and freedom. In this drama of deteriorating human relationships, the lyrical evocation of the ideal is analogously distorted and contradictory. Bernarda's relentless assertion of her authority, on the other hand, is based on a self-inflicted blindness to the intensifying crisis over the marriage of Angustias to El Romano, and when that crisis is too obvious to ignore, her tactic becomes one of outright repression: 'I have five chains for you, and this house my father built, so not even the weeds will know of my desolation' (*3 Trs*, 190). 'I was born to have my eyes always open. Now I'll watch without closing them 'till I die' (*3 Trs*, 194).

'Destiny' as it is represented in this play is not mysterious or cosmic in its dimensions, nor is it a part of an inscrutable but natural order that determines human lives. 'Nature', in fact, plays almost no part at all in the lives of these characters, except in the insidious guise of the erotic energy that drives Adela to her final rebellion. The circumstances of the daughters' lives are determined by the tradition and the custom of their class, and their limitation and suffering are caused by their Mother's inflexible imposition of conventions that have lost all meaning: 'For the eight years of mourning, not a breath of air will get in this house from the street', she declares to her daughters at their father's funeral, 'we'll act as if we'd sealed up doors and windows with bricks. That's what happened in my father's house – and in my grandfather's house' (*3 Trs*, 164). Bernarda is driven by her instinct to perpetuate the mores of her class and her family, and to do this, she must ignore all considerations of an emotional or subjective nature. The fanaticism with which she imposes and enforces these conventional strictures on conduct and expression is extreme in direct proportion to the extremity of Adela's rebellion against them. The isolation of Bernarda's family is only emphasised by the instances of depraved or desperate conduct on the part of people outside that become known either by rumours or by outbursts in the streets that penetrate the fortress-like walls of the house. The symbolic juxtaposition is that of a threatening and morally chaotic world outside, and a formal order that precariously controls potentially violent conflict inside.

Adela's struggle quickly becomes one of a clash of wills, as all members of the household conspire to prevent her from escaping. The action is structured around a series of confrontations between Adela and her mother, her sisters and the serving woman, La Poncia. The depth of Bernarda's tyranny and the extent to which the façade of public morality determines behaviour is seen in La Poncia's contradictory collaboration in Bernarda's authoritarian project. The play's entire first scene is devoted to the two servants, La Poncia and the Servant, who express their violent hatred of Bernarda, her deceased husband and her entire class. La Poncia's survival is dependent on her duplicitous and servile conduct: '. . . I'm a good watch dog! I bark when I'm told to and bite beggars' heels when she sics me on 'em. My sons work in her fields, both of them already married, but one of these days I'll have enough . . . Then I'll lock myself up in a room with her and spit in her face – for a whole year' (*3 Trs*, 159). Yet, when she attempts to stop Adela from seeing El Romano, she justifies herself by saying that she is determined to finish her days in a household whose honour has not been tainted by an illicit love affair. Not only do the daughters eagerly co-operate in locking the Grandmother away, but they collaborate to stop Adela. The oppressor's corruption affects the consciousness even of the oppressed and turns them against any expression of individual will to rebellion.

By his careful attention to the structure of each act, Lorca emphasises the thematic motif of surface versus depth, of that which is seen versus that which is hidden. Acts one and two both end with the dramatic tension at a high level, the first as the daughters forcibly subdue the Grandmother and return her to her locked room, and the second as all the women in the house – except Adela – join in the violent public persecution of a young woman who has killed her illegitimate child. Each following act begins, on the other hand, with scenes of exceptional tranquillity and surface composure: the servants alone in the opening scene, the daughters working embroidery and gossiping with the maid in act two, scene one, and the quiet supper with the neighbour Prudencia as the guest of the family which opens act three. The development of act three is following an established pattern, as the surface calm is steadily undermined, and the action builds toward the final violent confrontation which leads to Adela's suicide. Bernarda's command of 'silence!' that ends the play suggests the reassertion of her dominance that will restore the precarious and superficial calm of the house. As La Poncia has said to the Servant in the gloom of the final night-time scene, only moments before the definitive outburst, 'You feel this silence? – in each room there's a thunderstorm – and the day it breaks, it'll sweep all of us along with it' (*3 Trs*, 203).

The constant tension of this succession of scenes involving confrontation and dialogue that is charged with innuendo and hidden intention demands that a steady, relentless pace be established in performance. Juan Antonio Bardem, director of the 1964 Madrid production, even wished to eliminate in so far as possible the time

elapsed between acts, making the play a single, uninter-
rupted and uniformly paced unit.

In a symbolically parallel pattern, as the action moves
toward the crisis and catastrophe of the final scene, each act
calls for the action to take place in a space that is deeper and
deeper within the recesses of the house: act one is in a
sitting room, with arched doorways, from which church
bells outside can be heard, and it is brightly lit to emphasise
the shining and immaculate surfaces; act two is in an
interior room with exits that lead only deeper into the
house, to the bedrooms; act three is at night and is placed in
the area at the centre of the house, the interior patio. This
final act is played throughout in an increasing gloom as the
family retires after their late evening supper. The darkness
symbolically accompanies the death of the rebellious
daughter, Adela, and the reassertion of Bernarda's absolute dominance.

In this play, whose most prominent formal characteristic
is the discipline and the severity of its style, even the
symbolic terms of the action seem to be constricted and
diminished by the moral desolation of the society represented. The sense of crisis that is projected at the same time
gives the drama its exceptional power to engage and move
an audience. It is a drama of harsh oppression and of
victims, of tragic sacrifice rather than idealistic heroism.
The pathos of Adela's situation is that the only terms in
which she can conceive of her freedom are so woefully
compromised and dependent: escape from her mother's
tyranny promises only the life of an outcast woman, the
concubine of her sister's husband. The male – who never
appears onstage – is as much a symbol of oppression and
exploitation as is Bernarda. Adela's youth, and her
superior strength of will, make her unable to resign herself
to a future in her mother's house, and at the same time, give

her the desperate courage to rebel against her parent and the dehumanised morality she represents. Lorca's tragedy shows that the violence with which conventional morality is imposed and defended is a measure of its decadence and decline. The elimination of rebellion and the perpetuation of an oppressive ideology is achieved, not by direct physical violence (as is the case with the imprisonment of the Grandmother), but by the perverse distortion of the truth that provokes Adela to commit the ultimate violence against herself. Martirio's destructively motivated and jealous lie that El Romano has been shot by Bernarda as he attempted to flee from the discovery of his meeting with Adela stands as the culmination of the veiled hostility and intentionality that characterises the dialogue throughout the play. The consequences of this tense verbal aggression and its repressed violence are at last fatal.

The House of Bernarda Alba, with this relentless examination of the dynamics of oppression and the tragic consequences of a systematic suffocation of the human spirit, is Lorca's most highly developed response to his own call for a theatre committed to the exposure of the struggles and conflicts of his times. During the Franco regime in Spain, a great deal was made of Lorca's non-involvement in politics; the non-political nature of his writings was asserted again and again. In some cases, this constituted a well-intentioned effort to 'rehabilitate' Lorca by 'neutralising' him in such a way that he could not continue to be attacked and censored for political reasons by the dictatorship. While this restoration of stature was in part successful – and mainly where his poetry was concerned – it succeeded at the same time in purposefully obscuring an extremely important aspect of Lorca's activity and expression during the Second Spanish Republic, and particularly during the rising state of crisis that marked the Popular Front campaign of the winter of 1936.[5] *The House of Bernarda Alba* has been Lorca's most widely acclaimed and admired work for the theatre outside Spain since it was first performed in Buenos Aires in 1945; outside Spain, there has been little hesitation on the part of critics and commentators to call attention to the political significance of its symbolic structure. Moreover, there is now ample evidence that Lorca intended to move his theatre experimentally in the direction of the portrayal of political and ideological struggle when his life was so abruptly ended.

6
Innovation and Experiment

In 1936, Lorca referred to what he called his 'early' plays (*As Soon As Five Years Go By* and *The Public*) as 'unperformable'. He added, however, that these plays did exemplify the kind of work he really wanted to do in the theatre (II, 1016). Both of these highly experimental 'early' plays, and the one-act fragment, *Untitled Play* (1935 or 1936), are statements in practice of some of Lorca's most important insights into theatre as such, and are themselves explorations of the theatre's capacity to operate on many different levels other than those of logical dramatic discourse and 'realistic' representation.

As Soon As Five Years Go By was written sometime between 1929 and the summer of 1931 when Lorca read it out to a group of friends. *The Public* was also in progress at that time, and was probably finished sometime during 1930. After the performances of *Mariana Pineda* in 1927 and 1929, Lorca was working at one time or another on *The Love of Don Perlimplín* and on *The Shoemaker's Wonderful Wife* as well as on these two so-called 'unperformable' pieces. The adventure of his writing *The Public* and *Five Years* in 1929 and 1930 is all the more remarkable, given the fact that they are so divergent, not only from his previous works, but from his subsequent ones as well. It is doubtful that Lorca had any real hope that they would be performed and seen by any more than the same people who already constituted Spain's *avant-garde* of the late 1920s. Yet they represent the most concentrated assault that Lorca could have made upon the conventions of naturalism that dominated the stage at the time. In the farces, in *Don Perlimplín* and in the *Shoemaker's Wonderful Wife*, Lorca attacks these same conventions in favour of the free play of imagination and lyricism, but he does so in the light-hearted mode of the puppet theatre that calls attention to its own artificiality and that foregrounds the tension between naïve and self-conscious theatricality. Perhaps *Don Perlimplín*, with its merging of the pathetic and the grotesque, and its disregard for the strictures of surface realism, bears a closer resemblance to Lorca's experimental works than do any other of the comedies. Logical discourse begins to break down in these works and is replaced by sequences of scenes that produce the symbolic quality of dreams, both in their content and in their relationships to one another. The 'logic' of the subjective mind or of the dream prevails though we do not see the same abolition of all logic that was later to characterise European absurdist drama.

'As Soon As Five Years Go By' (1931)

Lorca called *Five Years* 'A Legend in Time in Three Acts and Five Scenes', and he referred to it as a 'mystery play that conforms to the characteristics of that genre, a mystery play about time'. Lorca's specific allusion to the traditional mystery play is particularly revealing. In the mystery, a tableau of symbolic characters would represent to the protagonist (the subject) scenes that were meant to reveal the workings of the human and the divine universe and to suggest the attitudes, values and actions appropriate to the protagonist's place in that universe. As was the rule in the medieval mystery plays, *Five Years* is illustrative and almost didactic in its concern with showing a fundamental truth about human life in its relationship to time, and ultimately, to death. All of the many and varied characters who appear onstage – the Old Man, The First and Second Friends, The Dead Child, The Cat, The Mannequin, The Football Player, The Harlequin, The Clown, etc. – are really the symbolic guises in which the Young Man's psyche dramatically presents to him the many aspects of the world outside himself. Not only that, but the world as it appears to him is constantly in flux, due primarily to the passage of time. Time, and its most definitive messenger, death, hover over everything and demand that the Young Man react and make choices under circumstances that cause him great anxiety. Paradoxically, however, no time at all elapses through the entire first act: the clock strikes six as the act begins, and it strikes six again as the act ends. Time, therefore, is shown to be something that is often felt rather than measured, although when life is contemplated in its relationship to death, time becomes both an objective as well as a subjective quality of experience, and a source of great dread for that reason.

The play's main subject – the Young Man – intends to marry his fiancée – the Betrothed – but will be able to do so only after a five-year period of waiting. Meanwhile, the Stenographer who works for the Young Man is shown to be desperately in love with him, but he constantly rejects her attempts to gain his attention. The Young Man, in fact, exhibits an extreme ambiguity of character that vacillates between his desire for the prompt satisfaction of his wish to possess the Betrothed, and the equally compelling pleasure of holding her image in his imagination where he can retain her in a state of perfection, suspended in time and space. The Old Man, with whom the Young Man has a mentor-pupil relationship, convinces him of the superiority of this interior realm of memory and imagination over that of the 'real' world:

> OLD MAN: . . . They change more, those things which are before our eyes than those which live without resistance within the mind . . .
>
> YOUNG MAN: Yes, yes. That which is inside is more alive even if it should also change.[1]

This hermetic and introverted stance is advocated by the Old Man, and it appeals strongly to the Young Man. It is challenged, however, by the intrusion of the two friends who represent polar opposites in their outlook and manner. The First Friend is the quintessential materialist. Whereas for the Old Man and the Young Man, anticipation is always superior to experience or possession, and the impossible and the ideal better than the real, for the First Friend, ego gratification and the satisfaction of appetite and impulse come before all else. The Second Friend, on the other hand, is regressive and sexually undifferentiated and he constantly seeks protection from the world, from time and from death in a series of womb-like or infantile refuges. So while the Old Man represents authority, there are other, conflicting psychic dispositions that make their claim on the Young Man's attention.

The scene that opens the second act reveals the extent to which the objective world fails to correspond to the Young

Man's world of imagination. When the Betrothed returns from her five-year cruise around the world, she begins a passionate affair with a Football Player who, in contrast to the insipid Young Man, is the ultimate masculine stereotype. The set represents a turn-of-the-century bedroom at night, with 'strange furniture' and clouds and angels painted on the walls. The Betrothed is inviting the cigar-smoking Football Player into her room for an amorous adventure before the Young Man arrives. As she kisses the Football Player, she says, 'What white heat! What ivory fire your teeth spill! My fiancé had icy teeth; he would kiss me and his lips would get covered with tiny dead leaves – they were dried lips. I cut off my braids because he liked them so much . . .' (*FLT*, 98). There follows the familiar scene between the Maid and the Betrothed where the young woman expresses her rage at the arranged marriage that is about to take place, and reveals herself to be an altogether different person from the one that the Young Man has been fashioning in his dreams. The Betrothed will, in fact, refuse to marry the Young Man despite the stern insistence of her father. This sequence of scenes is strikingly similar to one that occurs in *Blood Wedding*, only in that later play, it is reversed: The Bride, angry and increasingly desperate, is being readied for the wedding by her maid, when Leonardo intrudes into her house and they engage one another in a scene of intense but suppressed erotic power. When the Young Man enters after the Football Player has left, all the stage lights suddenly go up to their fullest brightness, as though he were waking from his five-year reverie all at once. He literally awakens to the fact that the Betrothed is not the Betrothed who has occupied his imagination over the previous five years. Typically, however, his anguish is due not to losing this specific person, but to being left with no object whatsoever upon which to focus the feelings of love he has cultivated so carefully in isolation in his own mind. The Young Man fears that he will suffer a psychic regression if the Betrothed refuses him, and even that he will die if this dream fails to materialise:

> YOUNG MAN: It isn't your deceit that hurts me. You're not evil. You mean nothing. It's my lost treasure. It's my purposeless love. But you will come with me.
> BETROTHED: I will not go.
> YOUNG MAN: So that I won't have to start all over again. I feel I'm forgetting even my ABC's.
> BETROTHED: I will not go.
> YOUNG MAN: So that I won't die. Do you hear that? So that I won't die. (*FLT*, 106–7)

With the Betrothed's disappearance, the Young Man is confronted by a Mannequin who comes onstage dressed in a bridal gown. She presents to the Young Man the promise that he will father a child in spite of his loss of the Betrothed. She is the Young Man's erotic fantasy, and her promise fulfils his desire to realise his own sexual role by producing offspring. As the act ends and other characters appear onstage, the Mannequin becomes rigid with a department-store-window pose. But when she is abandoned onstage as the curtain falls, the Mannequin's grief seems to indicate the impossibility of the birth of the child who might have been born of the union between the Young Man and the Betrothed. The Mannequin is the literal figuration of the absolute sterility of the Young Man's imaginary love. At the end of the scene, the Young Man has left in determined pursuit of the Stenographer, the new object of his love.

Abandoned by the Betrothed, the Young Man now

searches for the Stenographer in order to rekindle the love that she had felt for him in the past. Act three opens in a forest glade, surrounded by huge trees, in the midst of which stands a small baroque theatre. Harlequin enters, and it is he who will now direct the play's action from onstage. Harlequin is joined by The Clown whom Lorca describes as *'splendid'*, dressed in sequins and with a powdered head *'that gives the impression of a skull'*. He and Harlequin are powerful creatures who seem to control the entire stage now. While they offer to help the new lovers (The Young Man and the Stenographer) to find one another, they also mock their weaknesses and look upon the entire matter as a game and a ludicrous charade. Just as the definitive meeting between the Young Man and the Stenographer is about to take place, the curtains on the small stage are drawn back, revealing in miniature exactly the same set as occupied the main stage in act one, scene one. Now, in the small-stage representation of the library in the Young Man's house, a new encounter between the Young Man and the Stenographer is to take place under the direction of Harlequin and his assistant, The Clown. The Young Man and the Stenographer occupy the main stage alone, and they rhapsodise in verse about their love for one another. Then, they climb the stairs on to the second, smaller stage. Harlequin and The Clown appear to orchestrate the final moments of this scene within a scene. The Stenographer dreamily declares that her love is now something that goes far beyond the Young Man, and that it will take time for her to 'come down to' his level. In an exact reversal of the Young Man's rejection of her in the first act, she now declares that she will be his, only as soon as five years go by. The Young Man descends from the little stage, leaving the Stenographer in the ecstasy of her dream and the anticipation of love.

The final scene is played in the original library of the first act, which occupies the entire stage as before. It is clear now that the Young Man's time and his chance to love have expired. The rigid Mannequin is seen standing to one side, wearing the wedding gown, but without a head or hands. Three card players enter, formally dressed with long capes of white satin. On the wall of the library is the huge image of a human heart. The men engage the Young Man in a game of cards, and as they discuss among themselves the past victims of their game, it is immediately apparent that they have come to claim the Young Man in death. He grows increasingly anxious and desperate as the scene progresses and he tries a series of ploys to delay the finish of the game. But he cannot hold back the inevitable moment, and as he feels himself dying, he calls out to his servant; but we hear only echoes of his voice.

All through the drama, death has never been far away. Its most graphic representation occurs in the first act as the Young Man, the Old Man and the First Friend hide behind a screen and witness what appears to be at once a clairvoyant vision and a nightmare of the deaths of a Child and a Cat. The Dead Child, we later learn, is the son of the doorkeepers in the building where the Young Man lives. But the Dead Child is also emblematic of the swiftness and capriciousness of death itself. The Grim Reaper of the medieval mysteries does not actually appear on the stage (except in so far as the card players embody that traditional role), but both the Cat and the Child are literally snatched away off the stage and into the wings by hands that reach out and seize them. Moreover, the death of the Child suggests as well the death of childhood itself, which in psychological terms is the very transition or passage that the Young Man must make in order to resolve his ambivalence towards the world outside his imagination.

This point is foregrounded even more by the entrance of the Second Friend, a young male whom Lorca instructs could as well be played by a boy or a girl, in so far as he or she must project the sexual ambiguity of an ostensibly mature individual who has not made the transition out of childhood, and who clings to a world of infantile fetishes. The gathering storm outside the house prefigures the crisis to be suffered by the Young Man as he attempts to achieve the maturity and individuality necessary to love another. But he has cultivated the image of his absent fiancée for five years in his imagination alone, and has refused to acknowledge the love of the Stenographer who is with him every day. Time and death finally determine that the Young Man will never achieve his goals of love, marriage and fatherhood.

In *Five Years*, Lorca has used the space of the stage to play out in concrete terms the mystery drama of his protagonist's interior life in its dialectical relationship to his life in the world of other people. The empirical tests for separating interior from exterior, and imaginary from real, no longer apply from the standpoint of the spectator. Though the interpretation of the symbolic roles played by the generically-named figures in this drama may well be done through the methodologies of contemporary literary criticism, Lorca's conception of this work was thoroughly theatrical. The illusory but seductive comforts of fantasy and regressive escapism are symbolically played out on-stage, as are the contrastive roles of those who live in time, in the 'real' world and in constant struggle to seize the moment against the arrival of death. The Young Man is dramatically poised between these two spheres of consciousness, and finally, he loses the battle to insert himself successfully into the realm of the 'real'. Time and death conspire in the end to assert that the

Young Man has exhausted his opportunities to choose to live.

Lorca's 'mystery of time' also uses the stage to show and to make the public experience the profound tension between the discontinuity and irregularity of time as a subjective phenomenon on the one hand, and the simultaneous and ineluctible biological movement of time towards death on the other hand. Memory and imagination may ignore time altogether and thereby seem to defeat it, but the imagining subject continues to grow old and must die.

In the manner of allegory, the drama fragments the individual psyche and allows its various parts to struggle among themselves and with the world 'outside' the subject. The anguish of this struggle is the personal drama of the Young Man. *Five Years* is the drama of a personality in confrontation with challenges to transcend itself and its fantasy world and to grow. It is certainly one of the most striking examples of what Lorca meant when he talked about theatre being the place where poetry rises up off the page to become human, and where humans wear the garb of poetry, while at the same time, their bones and their blood show through for all to see. *Five Years* in fact may well be the authentic 'theatre beneath the sand' that was the subject of *The Public*, a play that Lorca was working on almost simultaneously with this one, from 1929 until summer 1931. Lorca, of course, knew that there was virtually no audience for this theatre in Spain, and thus he set these works aside, revising them only sporadically over the next several years.

Innovation and Experiment

'The Public'[2] (1931 and 1936)

Between 1929 and 1931, Lorca finished *Don Cristóbal's Puppet Show* and *The Shoemaker's Wonderful Wife*, where evidence of his experimental thinking about the theatre can be found in the prologues to the audience. In *The Public*, we have no friendly homily being delivered from the stage to the audience, however. Instead, we see the audience itself represented onstage by various characters who are engaged in provocative debate with the Director. The play itself, both in its form and its technique every bit as much as in what it 'says', is a challenging elaboration of Lorca's thinking about the theatre and its possibilities.

The theme of *The Public* is homosexual love, a relationship between human beings that Lorca also explored in his New York poetry from this same period (1929–31). But homosexuality is in a sense the lens through which Lorca focuses the theme of repression that is so prominent in its many different formulations in all of his work. In one form or another, the frustration of eros and the obstruction of instinctual passion are subjects in nearly all of Lorca's other plays. Here, the far more 'difficult' and even tabu subject of specifically homosexual love is brought to bear in a test of the limits of the theatre and of its public. To what extent – in 1930 and in Spain – would the theatre, its patrons and its audiences tolerate the exposition of these themes and subjects? Lorca accurately sensed what the answer to that question would be after the stunned and concerned reaction that his reading of the manuscript caused among his closest friends. Thus it was that later on, in 1933 in Buenos Aires, Lorca told an interviewer that *The Public* was a play he had no intention of producing in Buenos Aires, nor for that matter anywhere else, believing that no company would have dared to undertake it, and that no audience

143

would have stood for it. When asked why this should be so, he replied,

> because [the play] is the mirror image of the audience. That is, it causes the drama that each member of the audience is imagining to march across the stage, often without their taking notice of it, while they are watching the performance. And since the private drama of each person is at times extremely painful and generally not in the least way admirable, the spectators would rise up in their outrage and prohibit the performance from continuing. My play is not a work to be produced; it is, as I have defined it before, 'a poem to be hissed at'. (II, 929)

It is remarkable the extent to which this description of an anticipated audience reaction to the play corresponds to the audience reaction to a theatrical performance that is depicted in *The Public* itself. Along with incest (a theme that Lorca was possibly to deal with in his projected play, *The Daughters of Lot*), homosexual love was the love 'that dared not speak its name'. For that very reason, it was the theme that would figure in a play that was attempting to test and to push back the limits of the theatre and expand its expressive possibilities.

But homosexuality was only an aspect of love, one of its many and complex forms, according to Lorca's vision of this play. More fundamentally, erotic love, the power that draws one person to another, is represented in and of itself, as being altogether indifferent as to the identity of subject and object; it is a force that lies ultimately beyond human ability to channel and control. It is a force that is instinctual and natural; it is seen as part of an individual's destiny, and thus by definition, in dire conflict with the petty restraints and moral categories of bourgeois consciousness. Because society damns them, eros and homosexual love – while absolutely central to the play's conception and purpose – are also the means by which Lorca could formulate the problem of individual identity as one of dissimulation and disguise in opposition to authentic self-expression and self-disclosure. It is a problem that has always been at the heart of the phenomenology of the theatrical experience. But it was not Lorca's purpose in examining this theme to discover the ultimate absurdity of life in its resemblance to a vast dramatic production with everyone playing several different roles and wearing an unknown number of self-concealing and even hypocritical masks. Instead, Lorca seems to be intent in this play, as he is in his others, on revealing the alarming extent to which the repressive and dehumanising qualities of bourgeois culture have determined that certain human relationships are to be universally condemned. They are therefore driven underground where they are concealed from view, but their repression leads to their distortion and to the apparently anarchic energy with which they ultimately express themselves. Lorca goes on to confront the spectator with another experience whose reality is also repressed; it is the most isolating and solitary of all human experiences, but also the one that is universally shared: the experience of death.

The play opens in the study of the Director, and the final scene of the play returns to this setting, but with important alterations. As in *Five Years*, the apparent circularity of the play's structure and the fact that the final scene is one of symbolic death, contributes to the sense that the tableaux that we see here are really dramatisations of an inner as much as an outer crisis of consciousness and identity suffered by the Director himself. The Director sits in his study which is lit in blue; a huge hand is painted on one wall, and X-ray films take the place of windows, figuratively directing the gaze inward rather than outward. The Butler announces to the Director that the audience has arrived, and four white horses enter the study. But although the Director seems to be on intimate terms with the horses, he does not wish to see them. He sends them away, and the play begins again, as the Butler announces a visit by the audience. This time, three elegant and identically dressed Gentlemen enter. Over the course of this first scene, it becomes apparent that the Director has something to conceal. Although he speaks fervently about his innovative 'theatre beneath the open skies', the Gentlemen seem more interested in a theatre that they call the 'theatre beneath the sand', which would subvert the cowardly conventional theatre that they abhor. Their suggestions make the Director extremely anxious, and he protests that the audience would never tolerate such a radical departure from the norm as is suggested by the Gentlemen. He asks his visitors if they have brought with them a new play they wish him to consider but they reply that they themselves are the 'new play' and imply that the Director should recognise them even with their disguise beards and frock coats. The Director is now desperately trying to keep this play from taking further 'unexpected' turns, and he cries out for Helen to appear. But the First Gentleman has already set up a folding screen onstage and he forces the Director to pass behind it. The Director does so, and when he emerges from the other end of it, he is totally transformed, now wearing a suit of white satin with a white ruffled collar and carrying a tiny black guitar. Lorca specifies that this traditional Harlequin figure should be played by an actress.

Further transformations take place as the Gentlemen pass behind the screen. The Second Gentleman appears as a woman dressed in black pyjama trousers, with a crown of poppies on her head; in her hand she carries a lorgnette

with a blonde moustache attached which she will occasion-
ally raise to her face. Helen, the archetypal female siren,
now comes onstage, answering the Director's call. She will
engage in a struggle with the Third Gentleman, who has
been a homosexual lover of the Director sometime in the
past. His relationship with Helen has served the Director as
a heterosexual disguise before the rest of the world, but the
three Gentlemen are forcing him to drop the deception.
The Third Gentleman then passes behind the screen and
appears with chalk-white face, carrying a whip and wearing
gold-studded leather wrist bands. He beats the Director,
accusing him of constantly telling lies, while Helen declares
that she will not give in and will claim the Director for
herself. But the Gentlemen have certainly won, succeeding
in revealing the Director's secret and forcing his idea of the
theatre to pass to a new level of demystification and
authenticity. As the curtain falls, both the Director and the
First Gentleman (still in frock coat and beard) agree that
the play should begin.

The struggle in this drama is to be the Director's. His
'theatre beneath the open skies' has been for him an
adventure away from the traditional theatre, but he has not
gone far enough for the Gentlemen. These Gentlemen wish
to reveal for all to see and understand the essential nature
of erotic passion, and at this the Director trembles with
terror, knowing that the conventional audience would
destroy them were they to represent that truth. Not only
that, but the suggestion here is that only from the perspective of death can the real truth be apprehended and can
human life be seen unobscured by its unauthentic role-
playing and deception.

The subsequent scene is an allegorical tableau wherein
two sylph-like figures perform a choreographed dance and
dialogue that reveal their relationship to one another to be

one of love and aggression, dominance and subordination, tenderness and verbal as well as physical torture. The anguish of jealousy and abandonment is added as the 'Emperor' intervenes and chooses one of the two figures to be his own lover. Following this performance, which is witnessed by the Director and the Gentlemen onstage, the Director and the First Gentleman, in an analogous 'duet', address one another openly as lovers and engage in physical struggle. This dance scene of allegorical doubling appears to have caused the Director to relinquish his former false public identity.

Two plays by Shakespeare are brought into *The Public* and form an important part of Lorca's exploration of the limits of the theatre. The Director's 'theatre beneath the open skies' has just given a performance of *Romeo and Juliet*, and a 'revolution' has broken out among members of the audience as a result. They have discovered that the director had cast in the role of Romeo a thirty-five-year-old man, and in the role of Juliet, a fifteen-year-old boy. Outraged at this deception, the audience has hunted down the Director as well as the members of the cast. But there is disagreement over exactly what has so drastically infuriated the public. One Student from the audience alleges that the riot broke out when it was noticed that Romeo and Juliet were really making love onstage, rather than just acting. Another Student holds the opposite to have been true, that is, that the audience reacted to the discovery that the couple could never 'make love' since they were both males. Either the audience has objected to the drama's being too life-like, or they have objected to the drama's being too distant from their perception of life as it should be, and too much of a deception and an illusion. One Boy drives the paradox even further. He claims to have detected that Juliet was a male because he saw 'her' feet and noticed that they were too small, too feminine, too perfect to be real. In this case, the very perfection of the vehicle of illusion is precisely what discloses its fraudulence.

Whatever the results, the Director's intention with his 'theatre beneath the open skies' has been to demonstrate that it should make no difference what specific illusion may be used to awaken the public's feelings so long as those feelings are effectively aroused by the play. But here, the crude and materialistic curiosity of the audience has stripped away the power of the theatrical performance to convey truth by means of illusion. No matter how much the love scene may have moved the public's feelings, the fact that they have been 'deceived' by the Director's casting of the roles leads them to violent protest. One of the Students in the audience articulates the essential point that is being suggested by the debate:

Here lies the enormous error being committed by everyone alike, and the reason why the theatre is in its death throes. The audience ought not to cross over through the silks and the cardboard that the poet devises in his bedroom. Romeo could be a bird and Juliet could be a stone. Romeo could be a grain of salt and Juliet could be a map. What does it matter to the audience? (*Nadal*, 129)

And later, Student Two says: 'In the final analysis, do Romeo and Juliet have to be a man and a woman in order for the tomb scene to come off in a vital and moving way?' To which Student One replies, 'It is not necessary, and that is what the Director ingeniously set out to prove' (*Nadal*, 131). The Students celebrate the wonder of the illusion and attack the destructive desire of the audience to demystify the theatrical experience. The Director had bound and

149

gagged the 'real' Juliet and hidden her beneath a seat in the theatre. The audience, however, in its zeal for objective truth, has killed her in order to see whether there was someone else inside her, whether she was not perhaps just another simulacrum. 'And what have they got as a result?' one of the Students asks concerning the fanatic violence of the audience, 'A bunch of wounds and total disorientation' (*Nadal*, 139). As the Students leave the stage, their dialogue echoes an exchange that has been spoken before, in particular by the two allegorical figures, and by the Director and the First Gentleman: 'STUDENT ONE: . . . and if I want to fall in love with a crocodile? STUDENT FIVE: You'll do it. STUDENT ONE: And if I want to fall in love with you? STUDENT FIVE: . . . You'll do that too. I'll let you, and I'll carry you over the mountain peaks on my shoulders' (*Nadal*, 142–3). As they joyously proclaim this hegemony of feeling over form and of the emotion of love over the specificity of the subjects, the other members of the audience – the rioters – grope along fearfully through the gloom of the theatre, trying to find their way out.

In the final scene, after the other members of the cast have been killed in the riot, Death comes to the Director in the form of a Magician, dressed in black and wearing a long white cape. The scene, as at the opening of the drama, is in the Director's study, and the two men discuss what may or may not have been accomplished or resolved in this dramatic production. Although defeated in his attempt to revolutionise the theatre, the Director now looks back from the perspective of his own imminent death, and refuses to repudiate his experiment. Clearly, he has transgressed the limits of public tolerance, thrusting upon the audience a performance whose design was intended to prove an important premise about theatrical experience rather than to perpetuate their customary expectations.

The importance of the experiment lies in its ambition to confront the audience with an insight into their own behaviour and in its effort to prove a point about the power of illusion. The Director's experiment has been carried out in the play (*Romeo and Juliet*) 'within' this play (*The Public*), despite the fact that we do not see the performance in question, but rather witness its effects. What we see in addition are symbolic scenes that represent the subjective consequences of this experiment for the Director himself. He is confronted by the Three Gentlemen, who are disguised as members of the audience, but who also function as provocateurs and force the Director to push even farther than he had dared with *Romeo and Juliet*, into his own subjective confusion of roles and the repression of his own homosexuality in favour of an appearance that has gained him security and acceptance in the everyday world. So while the production of *Romeo and Juliet* provides the context for all that goes on in the play, it can also be said that *The Public* concerns the intimate anguish of the Director, who is suffering a severe crisis of identity. He is forced to examine his own hypocrisy and confusion, and ultimately to face his own death. Some of the figures in the play, it may be argued, are performing in the drama of the Director's subconscious mind; others seem to perform both in the world of the audience of his play as well as in the Director's interior world, while still others are entirely in the world of the theatregoers, the public.

In his discussion with the Director at the play's end, the Magician suggests that perhaps another Shakespearean play, *A Midsummer Night's Dream*, would have served more successfully to explore the themes; the key to its importance is the love of Titania for the Ass. Rafael Martínez Nadal, a friend of Lorca's, recalls a conversation he had with the poet in which Lorca mentioned his own particular view of the Shakespeare play: '[The scene with Titania and the Ass] is a scene filled with a tender lyricism and it must be played with the utmost seriousness', Lorca said,

> the comedy of the situation is meant for the audience, not the actors . . . Shakespeare wants to tell us that love does not depend on the individual, and it asserts itself with equal force on all levels. What happens in the forest [in *A Midsummer Night's Dream*] is what happens to all the characters whether under the magic spell of the fairies or not. . . . The key to the work is Titania who falls in love with the Ass. (*Nadal*, 234)

The Director seems to acknowledge that this play would indeed have conveyed the message, but he implies as well that his enterprise had turned out to be one of an even more radical nature, where the barriers between 'reality' and the stage were to be altogether abolished. This would be a theatre no longer based on the sleight-of-hand of dramatic illusion, but one in which what seemed to be happening onstage would be happening in reality; the Director declares that he spent days struggling to 'destroy the theatre . . . and to demonstrate that if Romeo and Juliet suffer and die only to awaken smiling when the curtain falls, [then] my characters, on the other hand, burn the curtain and die in fact, right in front of the audience' (*Nadal*, 155). The distinction between doing and representing, between the actual and the virtual, between reality and illusion would be abolished.

The suggestion that Lorca seems to be making here is not, of course, that we destroy the barrier between the stage illusion and the 'real' world. Instead, he is advocating that we acknowledge the barrier, that we recognise it – even while playing self-consciously back and forth across it – and finally, that we allow it to continue to set the world of the theatre apart as a space where symbolic actions can take place whose relationships to the lives of the spectators are as vital and concrete as are the events that 'happen' outside the theatre. The assault that Lorca is mounting here (and this is in 1930, before he had accomplished his major work for the stage) is arrayed against naïve naturalism, and against the assumption that theatre must at all costs create and maintain the illusion that what happens on stage is really happening, and is not merely the representation of actions and events. One of the Students in *The Public* defends the need for aesthetic distance after the Director's disastrous experiment in these terms: 'A spectator should never form part of the drama. When people go to the aquarium, they don't kill the sea snakes or the water rats, nor the leprous fish they see there, but they do let their eyes wander over the glass walls, and they learn' (*Nadal*, 139).

Lorca thus creates this drama about the creation of a drama that pretends to go beyond illusion; he shows the potentially chaotic consequences of this process, both when carried out in 'real' life – the dropping of disguises to reveal 'authentic' levels of being – and when attempted on the stage. The violence that ensues is perhaps the best indication of the conclusions that Lorca was reaching at the time concerning the possibilities of this kind of experimentation in his own work. The theatre's need to maintain an aesthetic distance from the public seems to be an implicit conclusion in this play. The fact that Lorca continued to struggle with these ideas is evidenced by the fact that only a few months before his death in 1936, he read what he called the definitive version of *The Public* aloud to friends in a Madrid cafe. He turned again to this set of problems in 1936, this time from a distinctly historical and political perspective, submitting his work for the theatre to a relentless examination of purpose and direction, in the fragment 'Untitled Play'.

'Untitled Play' (1936)[3]

The single act, called 'Untitled Play' confronts even more directly than *The Public* the problematic of the theatre and its limits. Lorca was writing 'Untitled Play' during a time of real crisis in Spain. Anti-government violence in the streets of Madrid was becoming increasingly frequent, and was spreading to other cities and to the countryside. Lorca spoke to friends during the spring of 1936 with a sense of great dread concerning the seeming inevitability of a bloody national conflict, but at the same time he demonstrated again and again his solidarity with the Republic and with its liberal ideology.

The problem of where his theatre was to find its voice, and to whom it would be directed became the subject of the 'Untitled Play', and in the fragment that we have, the question appears to be addressed from a specifically political point of view in order to focus on what are ultimately problems of the aesthetics of the theatre.

The first act (the only one we have) takes place in three distinct locations: first, on the stage proper, then among the audience in the theatre, and then finally, outside the theatre altogether. Characters who appear on the stage and who have a major part in the play are The Author, A Servant, and The Actress, who, besides playing herself, takes the roles of Queen Titania from *A Midsummer Night's Dream*, and Lady Macbeth. The minor speaking or walk-on parts are those of a Prompter, Nick Bottom from the Shakespeare play, a man dressed as a wolf, a Woodcutter, a Stagehand, and actors costumed as sylphs and faeries.

In the audience are The First Spectator and his wife who appear at the beginning, and The Second Spectator and his wife who appear at the end of this act; there is a well-dressed Young Man in an orchestra seat, the theatre owner (A Man Dressed in Black), and a Worker seated high in the balcony. Finally, the action outside the theatre is represented by the sounds of gunshots, artillery and a bombardment, as well as the voices of a throng of people in the streets.

The opening scenes of Lorca's farces are brought to mind as The Author begins the play on stage by himself in front of a grey backdrop, and immediately starts to berate the audience for their comfortably shallow and mediocre expectations in the theatre: 'Ladies and gentlemen', he declares,

> I am not going to raise the curtain in order to amuse the audience with plays on words, nor with a panorama showing a house where nothing goes on and where the theatre focuses its spotlight to entertain us and make us believe that life is really like that . . . You attend the theatre with the sole idea of being entertained, and you have writers whom you pay to do that . . . but today, the poet intends to take you prisoners because he wishes and aspires to move your hearts by showing you things you do not wish to see, by shouting out the truths that you do not wish to hear. (*Nadal*, 319–20)

But to certain spectators this is an attack which they refuse to accept passively. Such an assault on their consciousness in fact moves them to action as the First Spectator begins an aggressive debate with The Author from the floor of the theatre. The audience will accept theatre only if it represents an artificial, agreeable and

155

innocuous vision of reality. The Author, on the other hand, intends to destroy the conventional barriers that have rigidly divided the experience of the theatre from that of the world outside. The ideological and aesthetic terms of this conflict are the most important and interesting elements in this frustratingly abbreviated work. Not only do the public, as represented in this play, want to defend the isolated reality of 'their' stage, but they insist on the theatre's inherently superior capacity to evoke human emotion. Innured to the experience of their own lives, the public rely upon the artificial and vicarious stimulus of the theatre for their moments of strong feeling.

The Author insists on the need to open people's eyes to truths that cannot be represented in existing theatrical forms. He does not set himself the utopian goal of correcting human morality and behaviour through his art, but simply proposes to represent the truth in the theatre rather than illusion or deceit.

The focus of the play's polemic is The Author, while The Servant exemplifies the naïve spectator who may be entirely taken in by the false reality of the stage. The Actress soon appears onstage representing the individual for whom the theatre is the only reality there is, the person entirely dominated by illusion. The Author angrily objects to her coming out on stage for several important reasons. In the first place, it is clear that she is obsessed by her love for him and is pursuing him relentlessly. Second, in the eyes of The Author, The Actress embodies the pure sham and deceit of the conventional stage world. In fact, it appears that she cannot express herself at all unless in the artificial rhetoric of the traditional theatre: 'Lorenzo! Lorenzo!' she cries as she comes onstage dressed as Queen Titania and ready to rehearse *A Midsummer Night's Dream*, 'Why do you not come? I cannot work without you. And if I do not allow myself the pleasure of watching the sun rise nor run through the grass without my shoes, it is only to follow you and to be with you in these dark cellars' (*Nadal*, 339).

The Author also has significant ideological objections to presenting *A Midsummer Night's Dream*. While the play undeniably represents a true vision of love, The Author holds that its particular truth is terrible and distressing, and that it has no place in the world with which he is most concerned. Its truth is that love is entirely a blind force and ruled by chance. Love is shown by Shakespeare in this play to be a victimising rather than an ennobling power, leaving absolutely no choice or control over the matter to the individual involved. 'It is a terrible truth, but a destructive truth can lead to suicide, and the world, now more than ever, needs consoling truths, truths that are constructive' (*Nadal*, 343). The Actress at this point tries to change her own mind, and to join The Author in his revolutionary project, but she must confess in the end that she is too much in love with the fame and wealth that the conventional theatre offers her in return for pleasing the public. Disgusted by her remarks, The Author shouts furiously for her to leave the stage. Instead, she tries another theatrical role to see if it might come closer to the kind of truth he is seeking, or perhaps closer to the kind of woman he can love. She removes her white wig, uncovering long dark hair, and Queen Titania's white cape drops to the floor, revealing the scarlet robe of Lady Macbeth. She calls for the stage to be lit in red to accompany her representation of the mad scene. But The Author sees only deception and chicanery, and he demands that the stage be illuminated to full brightness and the house lights turned on as well.

At this point the principal rhetorical movement of the drama is towards the conclusion that the bourgeois commercial theatre must be transformed, even to the point of utterly destroying it. Just at this moment gunfire is heard outside the theatre. The reactions to this alarming development aggravate the already apparent divisions among the play's actors, both on the stage and in the audience. On the one hand, The Author calls for the theatre doors to be thrown open to allow the revolutionaries to enter: 'The theatre belongs to all', he proclaims, 'this is the school of the *pueblo*' (*Nadal*, 347). Others, on the other hand, frantically try to prepare armed resistance and a violent suppression of the popular uprising. From the audience, the Man in Black who owns the theatre calls for a bloody and horrifying revenge against the people in the streets. He justifies his call to arms by invoking the cliché ideals of bourgeois art: 'Gunpowder kills poetry', he claims at one point, '. . . goodness truth and beauty must have a gun in hand during these times' (*Nadal*, 349).

Through all this growing chaos, the wife of the spectator in the audience has been crying hysterically that the revolution has come, and that her children at home will be slaughtered by the mob. The Worker responds from the balcony that workers have never committed such crimes as she fears, but the woman's husband immediately tries to contradict him by citing an incident of such exaggerated atrocity that it can only be interpreted as totally untrue. His wife, obviously believing every detail, resumes her desperate cries about the terrible fate of her children. It is Lorca's final irony in this extensive opposition of the stage world to the real world to have The Actress irritably criticise the unconvincing way this mother in the audience is screaming about her children, and to offer her own ridiculously stylised theatrical version of how such a 'scene' should really be played.

At last, in the final moments of the act, the real world of

violence asserts itself over the world of the stage. When the Worker shouts out his support for the throng in the street who are demanding to be let into the theatre, he is shot dead by his antagonist, the Second Spectator. When the murderer dedicates his act to his unforgiving God, the tone of his speech is unmistakably that of the Christian fascist crusader: 'I am from God's army. My God does not forgive. He is the Lord of Hosts, to whom we must pay homage for strength, for there is no other truth' (*Nadal*, 357). The act ends with the entire theatre engulfed in flames, and The Author proclaiming the revolution's triumph.

In this untitled fragment, several important ideas concerning the theatre and its relationship to history are played out – the idea, for instance, that authentic theatre must not only respond to the movement of historical developments, but that it can actually participate as a progressive force in shaping those very developments. But does Lorca wish to suggest here the necessity of suspending the search for an ever-broadening and all-encompassing freedom for the theatre in favour of a theatre that would both reflect and orient people's will and spirit to the progressive struggles of that particular historical moment? This is the point of view that is so strongly displayed by The Author, and that seems to be in solidarity with the uprising that is in progress outside the theatre. It is certainly the boldest formulation of this particular idea in all of Lorca's known theatre.

The further question remains, however, as to whether Lorca might not have intended to refute this ideological point of view in the subsequent parts of the play, thereby defending the imaginative freedom that he had so eloquently upheld at other times. The possibility exists as well that Lorca could have intended to show that when the element of poetic illusion is eliminated from the theatre and is replaced by a naturalistic representation of reality, the stage is relinquishing its most effective means for reaching the public's consciousness. This would at least be consistent with the interpretation of Lorca's aesthetics derived from the discussion of *The Public*.

It is clear that this fragment represents a direct assault on the ideological, moral and formal assumptions of a theatre that was practically the private property of a dominant social and economic class – a class that from 1934 onwards in Spain was showing every sign of becoming violently reactionary. To judge from this untitled and incomplete piece, Lorca had chosen to bring ideological struggle on to the stage and into the audience with unprecedented force and directness. And he did not flinch from putting the traditional aesthetics of the theatre of imagination and poetry on trial at the same time. In 1935 and 1936 Lorca was seeking a theatre that would serve in its own way as a revolutionary force, and as an unprecedented provocation to artistic thought as well as action at that particular moment in Spain's history.

During the dramatic political, ideological and artistic ferment of the 1930s, Lorca was coming to see that art cannot ever be an indifferent or neutral phenomenon. The world of the Spanish theatre during the Second Republic, and the artistic world of Spain in general during Lorca's productive life were alive with the polemics raised by these questions. It is impossible to imagine that Lorca could not have been engaged constantly in their discussion or could have avoided organising his own thoughts and writing to respond to the important implications of these debates and to initiate new directions in the theatre.

The originality and boldness of these experimental plays are monuments to Lorca's imagination as well as to his artistic and intellectual discipline. Lorca the poet, Lorca the poetic dramatist, Lorca the human being living through extraordinarily critical times are all brought into exceptional focus in one of his final and most intimate interviews. In late 1935, he told his old friend the satirical artist, Bagaría:

> I listen to Nature and to Mankind with astonishment, and I copy what they teach me without pedantry and without giving things meanings that I can't really be certain that they have. Nobody, not even the poet, holds the secret of the world. . . . But people's suffering and the constant injustice that flows through the world, and my own body and my own thoughts prevent me from moving my house and dwelling away among the stars. (II, 1020)

Notes

1. Life and Literature

1. García Lorca, Federico, *Obras completas*, 2 vols (Madrid: Aguilar, 1975), Vol. II, p. 889. Parenthetical references to this edition will appear throughout the text citing volume number (I or II) and page.

2. Couffon, Claude, *Granada y García Lorca* (Buenos Aires: Losada, 1967), p. 25.

3. Couffon, p. 24.

4. Mora Guarnido, José, *Federico García Lorca y su mundo* (Buenos Aires: Losada, 1958), p. 25.

5. Jorge Guillén *Trece de nieve*, 2a época, núns. 1–2 (dic., 1967), p. 77.

6. Couffon, pp. 38–9.

7. Couffon, p. 74.

8. Rodrigo, Antonina, *García Lorca y Cataluña* (Barcelona: Planeta, 1975), p. 78.

9. The English title I will use for this play (*The Tragicomedy* . . .) is different from the one used by the play's translators (*The Billy-club Puppets*).

10. The English titles, *The Shoemaker's Wonderful Wife*, and *As Soon As Five Years Go By*, which I will use are different from the translators' *The Shoemaker's Prodigious Wife* and *If Five Years Pass*.

11. Fraser, Ronald, *The Blood of Spain* (London: Allen Lane, 1979), pp. 37–8.

12. Sáenz de la Calzada, Luis, *La Barraca: teatro universitario* (Madrid: Revista de Occidente, 1976), pp. 42–3.

13. Rodrigo, p. 396. José Luis Cano in *García Lorca* (Madrid: Ediciones Destino, 1974) asserts that Lorca was actually writing these plays (p. 20).

14. Gibson, Ian, *The Assassination of Federico García Lorca* (London: W. H. Allen, 1979). Gibson's is the most authoritative and best documented account of Lorca's last days in Granada and the circumstances of his death.

2. Lorca and the Spanish Theatre

1. Araquistáin, Luis, *La batalla teatral* (Madrid: Mundo Latino, 1930), p. 275.

2. O'Connor, Patricia W., *Gregorio and María Martínez Sierra* (Boston: Twayne, 1977), p. 32.

3. Ferreiro, Alfredo Mario, 'García Lorca en Montevideo', in Andrew A. Anderson, 'García Lorca in Montevideo: Un testimonio desconocido y más evidencia sobre la evolución de *Poeta en Nueva York*', *Bulletin Hispanique*, 83, nos. 1–2 (January–June 1981), p. 157.

3. The Comic Theatre

1. García Lorca, Federico, *Cinco farsas breves* (Buenos Aires: Losada, 1953), pp. 7–10.

2. Menarini, Piero, 'Les deux versions de *L'Idylle Sauvage de Don Cristóbal et de la Señá Rosita*,' *Europe* (August–September 1980), pp. 83–95.

3. Lorca, 'El estreno de *La Zapatera prodigiosa*', *La nación* (Buenos Aires), 30 November 1933.

4. The longer version is the one on which the Graham-Luján and O'Connell translation is based in *Five Plays* . . .

5. Lorca, 'El estreno de *La Zapatera prodigiosa*', *La nación*.

6. García Lorca, Federico, *Five Plays: Comedies and Tragicomedies*, tr, by James Graham-Luján and Richard L. O'Connell (New York: New Directions, 1963), p. 103. To be cited parenthetically in the text as *5 Plays*.

7. Allen, R. C., *Psyche and Symbol in the Theater of Federico García Lorca* (Austin: University of Texas Press, 1974). The best psychological (Jungian) criticism on Lorca's work.

Notes

4. The Granada Plays

1. Rodrigo, *García Lorca en Cataluña*, p. 373.
2. Rodrigo, pp. 64–5.
3. Rodrigo, p. 65.
4. Rodrigo, p. 100.
5. I have slightly changed the verse translation of this poem that was published in the Graham-Luján and O'Connell *Five Plays*, p. 136.
6. The Spanish word *cursilería* indicates pretentious and affected taste, particularly when vulgar and overstated; it is associated especially with the socially ambitious but unrefined petty-bourgeoisie in Spain.
7. García Lorca, Federico, *Three Tragedies by Lorca*, tr. by James Graham-Luján and Richard L. O'Connell (New York: New Directions, 1955), p. 13. To be cited parenthetically in text as *3 Trs*.
8. The verse translation is slightly changed from the Graham-Luján, O'Connell version, *5 Plays*, p. 171.
9. Allen, R. C., *Psyche and Symbol in the Theater of Federico García Lorca* (Austin: University of Texas Press, 1974). The best psychological (Jungian) study of Lorca's work.

5. The Three Rural Dramas

1. García Lorca, Federico, *El público y Comedia sin título*, R. Martínez Nadal and Marie Laffranque (eds) (Barcelona: Seix Barral, 1978), p. 19. To be cited in text as *Nadal*.
2. García Lorca, Federico, *Bodas de sangre* (Barcelona: Aymá, 1971), p. 66.
3. Sánchez, Robert, *García Lorca* (Madrid: Jura, 1950), p. 68.
4. Rubia Barcia, J., 'El realismo mágico en *La casa de Bernarda Alba*', in *Federico García Lorca*, Ildefonso-Manuel Gil (ed.) (Madrid: Taurus, 1975), p. 383.
5. This aspect of Lorca's life and work is clearly outlined by the poet's late brother Francisco in *Federico y su mundo*, by Francisco García Lorca (Madrid: Alianza Editorial, 1980), 'The Human and Political Commitment of García Lorca', pp. 401–18.

6. Innovation and Experiment

1. García Lorca, Federico, *From Lorca's Theater: Five Plays*, tr. by Richard L. O'Connell and James Graham-Luján (New York: Scribners, 1941). p. 79. To be cited in the text as *FLT*.

Notes

2. Translations from the text edited by Martínez Nadal are my own.

3. Translations from the text edited by Marie Laffranque and published in the Martínez Nadal volume are my own.

Bibliography

Plays by Lorca in Spanish

García Lorca, Federico, *Bodas de sangre* (Barcelona: Aymá, 1971).
García Lorca, Federico, *La casa de Bernarda Alba* (Barcelona: Aymá, 1964).
García Lorca, Federico, *Mariana Pineda y Doña Rosita la Soltera* (Madrid: Espasa Calpe, 1971).
García Lorca, Federico, *Obras completas*, 2 vols (Madrid: Aguilar, 1975).
García Lorca, Federico, *El público y Comedia sin título*, R. Martínez Nadal y Marie Laffranque (eds) (Barcelona: Aymá, 1973).
García Lorca, Federico, *Yerma* (Barcelona: Aymá, 1973).

Plays by Lorca in English Translation

Collected Plays, tr. by James Graham-Luján and Richard O'Connell (London: Secker and Warburg, 1976); *The Butterfly's Evil Spell*; *The Billy Club Puppets*; *The Shoemaker's Prodigious Wife*; *Don Perlimplín*; *Blood Wedding*; *Yerma*; *Doña Rosita the Spinster*; *The House of Bernarda Alba*.
Five Plays by Lorca: Comedies and Tragicomedies, tr. by James Graham-Luján and Richard L. O'Connell (Harmondsworth, England: Penguin, 1976; New York: New Directions, 1963, and Westport, Connecticut: Greenwood Press, 1977; *The Billy-Club Puppets*; *The*

Bibliography

Shoemaker's Prodigious Wife; *The Love of Don Perlimplín and Belisa in the Garden*; *Doña Rosita the Spinster*; *The Butterfly's Evil Spell*. Editions include scores of Lorca's original music for some of the plays.

From Lorca's Theater: Five Plays, tr. by Richard L. O'Connell and James Graham-Luján (New York: Scribners, 1941); *Yerma*; *If Five Years Pass*; *Doña Rosita*; *Don Perlimplín*; *The Shoemaker's Prodigious Wife*.

Three Tragedies by Lorca, tr. by James Graham-Luján and Richard W. O'Connell (New York: New Directions, 1955); *Blood Wedding*; *Yerma*; *The House of Bernarda Alba*. Introduction in English by Lorca's brother, Francisco García Lorca.

Three Tragedies: 'Yerma', 'Blood Wedding', 'The House of Bernarda Alba', tr. by Sue Bradbury; illus. by Peter Pendry (London: Folio Society, 1977).

Works on Lorca's Theatre and its Context

Adams, Mildred, *García Lorca: The Playwright and Poet* (New York: Braziller, 1977).

Allen, R. C., *Psyche and Symbol in the Theater of Federico García Lorca* (Austin, Texas: Univ. of Texas Press, 1974). Studies of *Don Perlimplín*, *Blood Wedding* and *Yerma*.

Auclaire, Marcelle, *Vida y muerte de García Lorca* (México: Ediciones Era, 1972).

Barea, Arturo, *The Poet and His People* (London: Faber and Faber, 1944).

Bentley, Eric, 'The Poet in Dublin', in his *In Search of Theater* (New York: Knopf, 1953). Concerns the Abbey Theatre production of *The House of Bernarda Alba*, staged by Eric Bentley, 1950.

Cano, José Luis, *García Lorca* (Madrid: Ediciones Destino, 1974).

Cobb, Carl, *Federico García Lorca* (New York: Twayne, 1967).

Couffon, Claude, *Granada y García Lorca* (Buenos Aires: Losada, 1967).

Durán, Manuel (ed.), *Lorca* (Englewood Cliffs, New Jersey: Prentice-Hall, 1962). Essays on life and works.

Edwards, Gwynne, *Lorca: The Theatre Beneath the Sand* (London: Marion Boyars, 1980).

García Lorca, Federico, *Deep Song and Other Prose*, tr. by Christopher Maurer (New York: New Directions, 1980). Of special interest are 'Elegy for María Blanchard', 'A Talk About the Theater' and 'Conversation with Bagaría'.

García Lorca, Federico, 'The Authority of the Theatre', tr. by Albert E. Sloman, in *The Modern Theatre*, Robert W. Corrigan (ed.) (New York: Macmillan, 1964), pp. 658–9.

García Lorca, Francisco, *Federico y su mundo* (Madrid: Alianza Editorial, 1980).

Bibliography

Gibson, Ian, *The Assassination of Federico García Lorca* (London: W. H. Allen, 1979).

Gil, Ildefonso-Manuel (ed.), *Federico García Lorca: El escritor y la crítica* (Madrid: Taurus, 1973).

Honig, Edwin, *Federico García Lorca* (London: Jonathan Cape, 1968).

Lima, Robert, *The Theater of García Lorca* (New York: Las Américas, 1963).

Martínez Nadal, Rafael, *Lorca's 'The Public': A Study of His Unfinished Play 'El público' and of Love and Death in the Works of Federico García Lorca* (London: Calder and Boyars: Lyrebird Press, 1974). Includes English translations of the play's text as established by M. Nadal.

Monleón, José, *García Lorca: Vida y obra de un poeta* (Barcelona: Aymá, 1974).

Mora Guarnido, José, *Federico García Lorca y su mundo* (Buenos Aires: Losada, 1958).

Rodrigo, Antonina, *García Lorca y Cataluña* (Barcelona: Planeta, 1975).

Ruiz Ramón, Francisco, *Historia del teatro español*, vol. 2 (Madrid: Alianza Editorial, 1971).

Sáenz de la Calzada, Luis, *La Barraca: Teatro universitario* (Madrid: Revista de Occidente, 1976).

Index

Abyssinia, 20

Albéñiz, Isaac, 8, 39

Alberti, Rafael, 4

Alfonso XIII (of Spain), 13

allegory, 142

Alvarez Quintero, Serafín and
  Joaquín, 24

Andalusia, 3, 7, 8

Aragón, Louis, 4

Arniches, Carlos, 24

As Soon As Five Years Go By
  (*Así que pasen cinco años*),
  12, 18, 21, 37, 133,
  134–42, 145

Azorín, *see* Martínez Ruiz,
  José

Bagaría, 161

Barcelona, 3, 10, 18, 19, 20,
  33, 73, 74

Bárcena, Catalina, 9

Bardem, Juan Antonio, 121,
  129

La Barraca, 15, 16–17, 18,
  20, 29–32, 84

Barrie, James, 27

Benavente, Jacinto, 23, 24

The Billy-Club Puppets, see
  *The Tragicomedy of Don
  Cristóbal and Mam'selle
  Rosita*

Blood Wedding (*Bodas de
  sangre*), 17, 18, 33, 37, 84,
  87, 88–9, 105, 112, 116,
  117, 119–20, 122, 137

Bonaparte, Joseph, 67

Book of Poems, see *Libro de
  poemas*

Breton, André, 4

Buenos Aires, 3, 17, 19,
  33, 47, 48, 49, 73, 132,
  143

Buñuel, Luis, 4

*Buster Keaton Goes For a
  Stroll*, see *El paseo de
  Buster Keaton*

The Butterfly's Evil Spell (*El maleficio de la mariposa*), 6, 9, 27, 35

Cain and Abel, 87
Calder, Alexander, 4
Calderón de la Barca, Pedro, 15, 30, 31, 56
Canciones, 11
Cervantes, Miguel de, 8, 15, 30, 39, 49
Chekhov, Anton, 65, 85
chorus, 96, 98, 100, 104, 112–13, 126
Club Anfistora, 21, 32
The Cock, see *El Gallo*
cristobitas, 38, 48 *see also guignol*; puppet theatre
Cuba, 12, 13, 18

Dalí, Ana María, 11
Dalí, Salvador, 4, 8, 10, 72
The Daughters of Lot, see *The Drama of Lot's Daughters*
death, 97–8, 100, 101, 135, 140–1, 145, 150
Debussy, Claude, 39
Deep Song, see *Poema del cante jondo*
The Destruction of Sodom (*La destrucción de Sodoma*), 19, 87
Díaz, Josefina, 9
Domínguez Berrueta, Martín, 4
Don Cristóbal's Puppet Show (*Retabillo de don Cristóbal*), 12, 39, 40–8, 50, 55, 58, 63, 143
La doncella, el marinero y el estudiante (*The Maiden, the Sailor and the Student*), 9
Los dos habladores, 8
Doña Rosita the Spinster (*Doña Rosita la soltera*), 18, 20, 37, 65, 66, 73–86, 90, 114, 118, 119–20
The Drama of Lot's Daughters (*El drama de las hijas de Loth*), 19, 87, 144
Dumas, Alexandre, 27

Echegaray, José de, 23
eros, 58, 63, 89, 94, 98, 100, 109, 116–17, 124, 138, 143, 144–5

Falla, Manuel de, 7, 39, 40
fascism, 20–1, 33, 159
Fernández Almagro, Melchor, 71
Fernando VII (of Spain), 66
Five Years, see *As Soon As Five Years Go By*
Flamenco, 7
Franco, General Francisco, 21, 131

El Gallo, 8
García Lorca, Francisco, 39, 73, 75, 78, 89
García Maroto, Gabriel, 6
García Rodríguez, Federico, 1
Gasch, Sebastiá, 11, 72
Golden Age (of Spanish Literature), 18, 49, 67
Goldoni, Carlo, 27
Granada, 1, 2, 3, 4, 7, 8, 12, 21, 65, 67–9, 73

guignol, 3, 38, 39, 42, 44, 46
  see also cristobitas; puppet
  theatre
Guillén, Jorge, 5
Gypsy Ballads, see
  Romancero gitano

L'histoire d'un Soldat, 7
The House of Bernarda Alba
  (*La casa de Bernarda
  Alba*), 17, 21, 37, 73, 84,
  87, 88–90, 105, 118,
  119–32

Ibsen, Henrik, 27
If Five Years Pass, see *As
  Soon As Five Years Go By*
'Imaginación, inspiración y
  evasión' ('Imagination,
  Inspiration and Escapism'),
  11
Impresiones y paisajes
  (*Impressions and
  Landscapes*), 4
Indice, 6
Iphigenia, 11
Isabel II (of Spain), 26

Jiménez, Juan Ramón, 4, 6

Lady Macbeth, 154, 157
Libro de poemas (*Book of
  Poems*), 6
Lope de Vega, Félix, 15, 20,
  30, 56
Lorca Romero, Vicenta, 1
*The Love of Don Perlimplín
  With Belisa in the Garden*
  (*El amor de don Perlimplín
  con Belisa en el jardín*), 11,
  12, 18, 32, 57–63, 133, 134

Machado, Antonio, 4, 24
Machado, Manuel, 24
Madrid, 3, 4, 5, 10, 18, 19,
  48, 49, 153, 154
Maeterlinck, Maurice, 35
*The Maiden, the Sailor and the
  Student*, see *La doncella, el
  marinero y el estudiante*
*The Maiden Who Waters the
  Sweet Basil and the
  Inquisitive Prince*, see *La
  niña que riega la albahaca y
  el príncipe preguntón*
Manifiesto anti-artístico, 8
Mariana Pineda, 7, 9, 10, 12,
  65, 66–73, 75, 76, 133
Marquina, Eduardo, 24
Martínez Nadal, Rafael, 87,
  88, 151
Martínez Ruiz, José (Azorín),
  24
Martínez Sierra, Gregorio, 6,
  9, 26, 27
Martínez Sierra, María, 26
Mexico, 20
A Midsummer Night's Dream,
  151–2, 154, 156, 157
Molière, 27
Montesinos, Manuel, 21
Muñoz Seca, Pedro, 24
Mussolini, Benito, 20
*The Mystery of the Three
  Wisemen From the East* (*El
  misterio de los tres reyes de
  Oriente*), 7, 39
mystery plays, 7, 134–5, 140,
  141, 142

naturalism, 34–5
New York, 3, 12–13, 18, 48,
  143

Index

La niña que riega la albahaca y el príncipe preguntón (*The Maiden Who Waters the Sweet Basil and the Inquisitive Prince*), 8, 39
Nobel Prize, 23

El paseo de Buster Keaton (*Buster Keaton Goes For a Stroll*), 9
Pedrell, Felipe, 7
Pérez Galdós, Benito, 24
peripeteia, 96
Poema del cante jondo (*Deep Song*), 7, 14
Poeta en Nueva York (*Poet in New York*), 13, 14, 143
Primo de Rivera, General Miguel, 9, 12, 13, 25
The Public (*El público*), 12, 18, 37, 133, 142, 143–54, 160
puppet theatre, 38–41 *see also guignol*; *cristobitas*

Ravel, Maurice, 39
Republic, Second Spanish, 13–14, 15–16, 17, 21, 30, 84, 131, 154, 160
Residencia de Estudiantes, 4–5
Ríos, Fernando de los, 4, 12, 16
Romancero gitano (*Gypsy Ballads*), 7, 11
Romeo and Juliet, 148, 149–50, 151
Rueda, Lope de, 30

Sala, Grau, 74

Salazar, Adolfo, 6
La sangre no tiene voz (*Blood Has No Voice*), 18
Shakespeare, William, 27, 148, 151
Shaw, George Bernard, 27
The Shoemaker's Wonderful Wife (*La Zapatera prodigiosa*), 12, 14, 18, 32, 37, 48–57, 63, 133, 134, 143
Songs, see *Canciones*
Stravinsky, Igor, 4, 7, 39

Teatro Eslava, 26–7, 66
Teatro Goya, 121
The Three Wisemen, see *The Mystery of the Three Wisemen From the East*
Tirso de Molina, 15, 30, 56
Torre, Guillermo de, 38
tragedy, 88, 89, 93, 96–7, 99, 101, 102, 103, 104, 105, 106, 117, 118, 120, 122, 123 (romantic), 130, 131
The Tragicomedy of Don Cristóbal and Mam'selle Rosita (*Los títeres de cachiporra: La tragicomedia de don Cristóbal y la Señá Rosita*), 11, 40–8, 50, 55, 63

Ugarte, Eduardo, 16
Unamuno, Miguel de, 24
'Untitled Play' ('Comedia sintítulo'), 37, 133, 154–60

Valery, Paul, 4
Valle-Inclán, Ramón María del, 25–6

Wells, H. G., 4

Yeats, William Butler, 35
Yerma, 17, 18, 20, 37, 73, 76,

84, 87, 88–9, 103–19,
119–20
Xirgu, Margarita, 10, 14, 18,
20, 71, 73